MONASTERIALES INDICIA

The Anglo-Saxon Monastic Sign Language

Edited with notes and translation by

Debby Ba

Anglo-Saxon Books

Published by
Anglo-Saxon Books
25 Malpas Drive
Pinner
Middlesex
England

Printed by
Antony Rowe Ltd.
Bumper's Farm
Chippenham
Wiltshire
England

First Published 1991
Reprinted 1993

ISBN 0-9516209-4-0

ACKNOWLEDGEMENTS

I should like to thank the many friends and colleagues who have helped me with various aspects of my work on the *Monasteriales Indicia*, particularly David Sherlock for several conversations about the text, and information on other sign languages, Bill Zajac for discussing later sign language, Dr Sarah Foot for information about early English monasticism, Dr Sue Edgington and Frank Goodingham for reading the work in draft, and Marilyn Thompson of Heffer's bookshop, without whom this book would not have been published. I am also grateful to the staff of Cambridge University Library and the British Library, both the Reading Room and the Manuscripts Department, for their help.

Debby Banham
May Day 1991

CONTENTS

INTRODUCTION

Monastic Reform and Monastic Sign Language

It would be impossible to follow the Rule of St Benedict, with its insistence on silence, not only in church, but also at table and at night, without some means of non-verbal communication.[1] In fact, St Benedict prescribed that his monks should use signs, rather than speaking, if they needed anything at mealtimes,[2] but it is not known whether a recognizable sign language developed in Benedict's own lifetime. The earliest surviving texts are associated with the Benedictine reform movement of the tenth century, 400 years after St Benedict's time, and especially with that branch of the movement which began at the monastery of Cluny in Burgundy, founded in the year 910.

The reform movement reached England in the time of King Edgar (959-975), and the Old English sign language, or *Monasteriales Indicia,* edited here may date back to that reign. It is found in the mid-eleventh century British Library manuscript Cotton Tiberius A.III, from Christ Church, Canterbury, the Cathedral. This manuscript is clearly a product of the Benedictine reform, for it contains a copy of the Rule of St Benedict, and one of only two copies of the *Regularis Concordia,* the English reformers' 'agreement about the rule', both glossed in Old English, as well as a number of other texts of monastic interest. It also contains two full-page illustrations, one showing King Edgar flanked by the reforming bishops Æþelwold and Dunstan, with a monk below, prefacing the *Concordia,* and one of St Benedict presenting his Rule to his monks, or perhaps the other way round, prefacing the Rule itself.[3] The manuscript thus emphasizes, pictorially as well as in its selection of texts, the uniformity of reformed

---

[1] see *RSB*, chapters 6, 38, 42 *et passim.*
[2] chapter 38.
[3] reproduced in Temple, no.100.

English monasticism, its Englishness and its dependence on royal patronage.

It is not absolutely certain that Tiberius A.III was written at Christ Church, but it belonged there later in the Middle Ages, and Christ Church, as well as being the metropolitan see, was an important centre of the English reform movement. It was the seat of the monk-bishop Oda (941-58), who had received the tonsure at the reformed house of Fleury in France, and then of Dunstan (959-88), the former abbot of Glastonbury and one of the three leaders of the reform under Edgar. The community serving Christ Church, which previously had been at least partly made up of canons, who were allowed to marry and to own property, became a reformed Benedictine monastery, either in Dunstan's time or under one of his immediate successors, who were all monks themselves.[4]

To what extent silence was observed in pre-reform English monasticism, in which the Rule of Benedict was certainly known, but was not regarded as binding, or taking precedence over any of the other rules available, it is impossible to tell.[5] Where silence was considered important, some kind of sign language may well have been in use before the Benedictine reform, but no codification of it survives. In fact, the similarity of the Old English *Indicia* to the earliest continental codes makes it likely that our text is a translation of a Latin sign-language introduced from the Continent at the time of the reform, or, more likely, a compilation, one of whose sources was such a continental sign list. Other sources may have included one or more lists already available in pre-reform England, signs already in use but not previously written down, or signs developed in England to

---

[4] see Brooks, chapters 10 and 11.

[5] Dr Sarah Foot, who has made a fundamental study of pre-reform English monasticism, has been able to find no evidence on this point.

augment the continental list. However, there is no other Anglo-Saxon evidence for the use of sign language.

The subsequent history of monastic sign language in England suggests, if somewhat tenuously, that monks in reformed English houses did make use of the *Indicia* in their daily life (see below), rather than simply copying it into their manuscripts. However, the careless and apparently uncomprehending way in which parts of the text are copied may argue against this, as may the fact that it has apparently not been adapted to conditions at Christ Church (it retains the sign for abbot, instead of introducing one for the archbishop, who fulfilled the role of abbot as overall head of the house).[6] On the other hand, it must be borne in mind that the other texts in Tiberius A.III are not specific to Christ Church either, and some of them, such as a charm for curing sick horses, are not even very monastic.

The oldest continental sign lists are in two customaries from Cluny, written by two monks of that house, Bernhard and Udalrich.[7] These two, writing in about 1075 and about 1083 respectively, and thus somewhat after the date of the manuscript of the English *Indicia*, present identical lists of signs, which must represent the sign language in use at Cluny in their time, or a text already available there. According to the *Vita* of the great reforming abbot of Cluny, Odo (926-944), sign language was already in use at the monastery of La Baume when Odo entered that house as a monk.[8] It seems likely, therefore, that the use of signs was introduced to Cluny either by Odo, or by his mentor Berno, the founding abbot of Cluny (910-26), who had also preceded him as abbot at La Baume. On the Continent, as in England, it is impossible to tell whether, or to what extent, sign language was practised before the reform movement got under

---

[6] I am grateful to David Sherlock for pointing this out to me.
[7] edited by Jarecki, no. 1.
[8] John of Salerno, *Vita Odonis*, chapter 32.

way. It seems on the face of it unlikely that it was invented *de novo* by Berno, who besides being an enthusiastic reformer was a major public figure, but he or Odo may have codified what were previously unsystematic attempts, at monasteries where the Benedictine prescriptions on silence were taken seriously, to communicate without speech.

Another early list is preserved in the *Constitutiones* of William, the reforming abbot of Hirsau in South-west Germany, of the late eleventh century.[9] His text is based on the Cluny *Consuetudines* of Udalrich, but contains a much longer sign list. Since William sent monks to Cluny three times to study the reformed way of life there, and since some of his signs, although not described in the Cluny list, are implied by the descriptions of others there, it is likely that his list represents the Cluny sign language of his time better than the lists from Cluny itself, which may have excluded unofficial signs or those that had come into use since the introduction of sign language there. The Cluny list may therefore be in origin a good deal older than the texts containing it, perhaps even going back to the foundation of the house in 910, or to the time of Odo.

Relationship of the Early Texts

The Old English *Indicia* contains a number of signs not found in the basic Cluny list, but over half of them are also found in William of Hirsau. This could be dismissed as mere coincidence, due to the fact that his list is by far the longest, but the descriptions of some signs (such as those for chalice and butter) are so similar as to suggest a common source, perhaps the putative eleventh-century Cluny sign language, whether it existed as a written text, or only as usage. This would make the *Indicia* later, as a list, than that preserved by the two Cluny writers, unless the enlarged Cluny sign language had evolved in the tenth century,

---

[9] edited by Jarecki, no. 3.

and the official list had become fossilized at a very early stage. If this was the case, the Old English *Indicia* could be a translation of, or compilation from, a text which reached England at more or less the same time as the reform, perhaps contemporary with the composition of the *Regularis Concordia*, but if not, the Cluny list, the *Indicia,* and William of Hirsau's list may represent successive stages in the expansion of Cluny sign language, and the text on which the Old English is based may not have arrived long before the date of the manuscript. However, the *Indicia* has evidently been copied into Tiberius A.III from another manuscript, since it contains a number of errors, some of them serious; some period of time, however short, must have elapsed between the translation or compilation and writing down of the extant version. For a piece of evidence for the Cluny - *Indicia* - Hirsau sequence, see note to sign 79, below.

Sign Language in England

The Old English sign list is the only early one in the vernacular. Presumably it was translated so that the signs could be taught to children, or indeed older entrants to the monastery, who did not yet have a good command of Latin. It may well be that the Anglo-Saxons found Latin harder to learn than did their continental contemporaries, some of whom spoke Romance languages still quite close to Latin. Interestingly in this regard, Tiberius A.III also contains a glossed copy of Ælfric's *Colloquy*, a set of dialogues designed for teaching Latin to monastic pupils.[10] This text contains information on Anglo-Saxon monastic life which complements and confirms that of the *Indicia*.

No sign lists survive from England in the period immediately after the date of Tiberius A.III. This is of course also the period of the Norman Conquest, which caused great disruption in, among other things, manuscript production. There are, however, four English

---

[10] edited by Garmonsway.

sign lists extant from the later Middle Ages. Two of these come from fourteenth-century Bury St Edmunds, but are not identical, one from Ely Cathedral Priory, again in the fourteenth century, and one from Syon Nunnery in the fifteenth century.[11] Of these, that from Ely is almost identical with a contemporary list belonging to the Victorine canons of St Thomas, Dublin, and the twelfth-century list from the Victorines' mother house in Paris. The Syon list is the only one in the vernacular, but the vast differences between the English of the fifteenth and eleventh centuries make it little easier to compare with the *Indicia* than the Latin lists.

Despite the passage of at least three hundred years, and the changes in monasticism during that time, there are striking similarities between the Old English *Indicia* and the later English sign lists, apart from the Ely text, which is copied faithfully from its Parisian original. About a third of those signs in the *Indicia* which do not occur in the Cluny lists, and which I have tentatively attributed to an enlarged Cluny sign language, do also occur in the two Bury lists, and in the one from Syon. This is only a matter of seventeen signs at most, but there are also a number of signs from the original Cluny list which are missing from the *Indicia*, and also from these three later English texts, but occur in most, if not all, of the continental lists.

The identity of these signs suggests that we are dealing, in most cases, with deliberate modification to suit English conditions, rather than carelessness or caprice. For instance, all signs for fancy types of bread are absent from the English lists, as is the sign for pancakes, although the signs for cheesecakes and pasties are found in the two Bury lists. Similarly, the Cluny sign for a

---

[11] The two Bury sign lists are edited by Jarecki (British Library ms. Harley 1005), no. 6, and Sherlock and Zajac (Cambridge University Library ms. Add. 6006). The Ely sign list, in Lambeth Palace Library ms. 448, is unpublished, but the Paris list on which it is based is Jarecki, no. 4. The Syon list is printed by Aungier, pp. 405-9.

drink flavoured with wormwood is missing, as are those for two items of bed-clothes, leaving only those for bed-cover and pillow. These omissions probably reflect a less sophisticated way of life in English monasteries, compared with their continental counterparts, at least at the date of the *Indicia*, while others, for books and for elements of worship, may be due to liturgical differences. The absence of most of the Cluny signs standing for verbs rather than nouns or adjectives must mean that sign language possessed a less complex syntax in England than on the continent.

Additional signs for objects pertaining to divine service, including 'chalice', presumably do not mean that such items were not familiar on the Continent. On the other hand, the sign for butter or fat, also found in William of Hirsau, may have been introduced to account for dietary customs in England and Germany which were not found at Cluny, or other southern houses (some of the continental lists do have signs for 'oil'). Only one additional sign, that for 'enough', is found in all four English lists and not in William, but I doubt that this tells us anything about differences between English and continental monasticism.

These connections between the *Indicia* and the later English lists suggest either a continuous tradition, in use, of a sign language adapted to English conditions, or possibly a textual tradition in England whose intermediate stages are lost to us (or, of course, a combination of both). Nonetheless, all the later English lists also contain signs from the Cluny list which are unknown to the *Indicia*, and omit most of the signs which the *Indicia* added to the Cluny vocabulary. This means that the compilers of the later lists, or of the sign languages on which they were based, must also have been familiar with parts of the Cluniac sign language tradition not transmitted through the *Indicia*. At what point these non-*Indicia* elements reached England cannot be established, in the absence of intermediate English sign lists, nor can we tell whether they arrived as text or practice. All we can say for certain is that English monasticism continued to use sign language, or at least continued to have some reason for producing and writing down sign lists.

Importance of the Text

Apart from the intrinsic fascination of knowing how monks coped with the limitations of silence a thousand years ago, the main interest of the *Monasteriales Indicia* is as evidence for the details of Anglo-Saxon monastic life. The Rule of St Benedict and the *Regularis Concordia* set out how monks ought to behave, and dwell at great length on the *opus dei*, the daily and annual cycles of worship, but the *Concordia*, especially, devotes little attention to such mundane matters as dress and diet. This means that there is very little evidence from England on these minutiae, or for how monastic life was actually experienced, as opposed to prescribed. Besides the *Indicia*, the main sources of information are the *Colloquies* of abbot Ælfric and his pupil Ælfric Bata.[12] One limitation of these is obvious: they were designed for teaching, not as an accurate record, although, at least in as far as life within the monastery is concerned, they could not have deviated too far from the truth without puzzling their readers considerably. Moreover, there would be little point in teaching beginners Latin words for things or practices they would not in fact meet. Less obviously, perhaps, the colloquies deal overwhelmingly with the lives of the *pueri*, not of adult monks. Although a character calling himself 'monachus professus' is introduced at the beginning of Ælfric's *Colloquy*, he tells us very little about himself. Where they deal with the same material, however, the colloquies and the *Indicia* very much support each other.

The *Indicia*, then, is unique in providing a picture of Anglo-Saxon monastic life not limited by the requirements of the classroom, or by a juvenile viewpoint. It could be objected that it is no more

---

[12] both printed in Stevenson, as well as, in abbot Ælfric's case, Garmonsway.

intended as a record than are the colloquies, but a similar argument applies to it as to them: the monks would not have bothered to devise or record signs that they were not actually going to use. Its relationship to the continental lists does of course mean that some signs may have been preserved which owe more to its Cluny sources than to English practice, but the large number of cases in which the *Indicia* adds to, omits, or modifies signs that were used on the continent, should inspire confidence that it reflects Anglo-Saxon, rather than continental, conditions. The preservation of some of its modifications in the later English lists reinforces this view. Of course, a high degree of similarity with the Cluniac lists should be expected, since the imitation of up to date continental practice was the whole point of the English reform. Where the *Indicia* differs, therefore, we are justified in supposing that late Anglo-Saxon monastic life also deviated from its exemplars.

Manuscript

British Library manuscript Tiberius A.III is the only manuscript of the Old English *Monasteriales Indicia*. It is a composite codex, of which the largest original unit (folios 1-173) contains the *Regularis Concordia*, the Old English glossed Rule of St Benedict and the other items mentioned above. Ker dates the script to the mid eleventh century, and identifies the manuscript with one in a twelfth-century catalogue from Christ Church, Canterbury, but does not say definitely that it was written there.[13] Temple, in common with art historians generally, regards this as a Christ Church product, presumably on the evidence of the illustrations. Dodwell describes Tiberius A.III as 'probably among the last illuminated manuscripts to be made at Canterbury before the Conquest'.[14] Nevertheless, the style of painting practised in such an influential ecclesiastical centre must also have been in use

---

[13] pp. xl and 240-8.
[14] p. 4.

15

elsewhere, especially when scribes or artists were sent from one house to another by their superiors.

Tiberius A.III appears to have been affected by the fire of 1731, in which so many manuscripts in the Cotton collection were damaged or destroyed, for the tops of all the folios are shrunken in a way characteristic of the effects of heat on parchment. However, the script is still legible in all but a very few places (none of them in the *Indicia*) where the top margin has entirely disappeared. The leaves have been individually mounted in paper, making the original construction of the manuscript difficult to establish. The present size of the folios is about 240 by 180 millimetres, varying by no more than 5 mm. The width is probably not greatly reduced from the original size; some trimming has certainly taken place at the outside edge, but a good margin (about 15 mm.) remains on the inside of most folios. The height of the pages, however, must have been substantially more; at least 25 mm. has probably been lost by shrinkage and the loss of the upper margin (probably by crumbling of the fire-crisped membrane), as well as some trimming at the bottom of the leaves.

The *Monasteriales Indicia* is found on folios 97 verso to 101 verso of the manuscript, with an opening rubric at the foot of 97 recto. To judge by the ruling, folios 96 to 103 formed an original quire, assembled with like side facing like, and the hair side on the outside. As well as the *Indicia*, this quire contains the end of a set of directions for a confessor, an Old English lapidary, a warning against pride, and the beginning of an isolated chapter of the Benedictine Rule; in other words, it does not form a thematic unit. The folios are ruled from the flesh side, with either 33 or 34 lines per page (33 on folios 96-7, 34 on 98, 33 on 99-100, 34 on 101, and 33 on 102-3). The lines are spaced unevenly, mostly at about 5 mm., with a particularly tightly squashed group about three quarters of the way down. The writing space is contained by double lines all round, again about 5 mm. apart. On the left hand side, the space between them is mostly empty, being used only for the initials beginning new paragraphs, but on the right, the writing often extends into, and occasionally beyond, this space. The top line is written on. No prickings are visible on these folios, although they do show a pair of holes either side at the top, which bear no relationship to the ruling, and some have a few holes at the outer edge, again apparently unconnected. The overall size of the writing space (including the top line of script) varies between 210 and 230 mm. in height, and 150 to 170 in width.

Although this is a presentation volume, containing important texts, as well as the two illuminated pages, the copying of the *Indicia* is bad, occasionally to the point of incomprehensibility. The whole quire was written in a small, irregular vernacular minuscule by a single scribe, Ker's no. 4, who continued to folio 107 verso, and also wrote several other sections of the book, including a Latin prayer. The descenders of the letters are generally very short, and the same is true of most of the ascenders, except those of the Old English letters *ð* and *þ*, in which they are taller. Ascenders are usually wedge-shaped, occasionally slightly forked. The top of *e* is occasionally open, as, less frequently, is *p*. The low *r* is sometimes almost closed underneath, making it look like a *p*. *s* is long, *a* and *d* low, and *g* 3-shaped. The Old English *æ* is used. Crossed *þ* is normally used for 'þæt', the Tyronian nota (7) is found throughout for 'and', and suspension marks occasionally occur over the ends of words, for final *m* and *n*. The ink is mostly a mid-brown, but varies from buffish to almost black, often due to changes in the surface of the parchment.

The initials were added in red after the main part of the text was written, and are occasionally omitted, or incorrect. The opening initial *Þ* is decorated with a pendant double curl, and extends to the height of three lines of writing; otherwise the initials are plain. The opening rubric is in small rustic capitals, and the closing one in Caroline minuscule. This enables us to see that the scribe has observed the distinction between insular and continental forms of *d*, *r* and *s*. The low insular form of *a* is used in the word 'monasteriales' in the closing rubric, but the high Caroline form in 'indicia'. This rubric is clearly by the same hand as the main text, and the same is almost certainly true of the opening rubric and the initials. Initials and rubrics are all in the same ink.

It does not seem likely that the scribe was unfamiliar with Old English, so the fairly numerous scribal errors can only be attributed to carelessness. As already mentioned, these errors in copying show that Tiberius A.III cannot be the original manuscript of the *Indicia*, but must be copied from it or an intermediate copy.

Editorial Practice

This is a semi-diplomatic edition, but it is intended to be a readable one. That is to say, since there is only one manuscript of the text, I have followed it, without any attempt at normalization, wherever there is no pressing reason to the contrary, but I have not preserved idiosyncrasies which would confuse a reader. Since the surviving manuscript is not the original, its readings have only scribal status, and cannot be attributed to the translator or compiler, but, except where they are quite manifestly wrong, they are the best guide we have to what the compiler's or translator's intentions might have been.

All manuscript readings emended in the text are shown in footnotes. I have kept the manuscript's spelling, even when it is quite strange, or apparently ungrammatical, except where it would render a word unrecognizable to someone with a reasonable command of Old English. Similarly, I reproduce manuscript word-division, although it frequently separates elements of a compound word, and only emend where it joins two words together or breaks a simplex (or element of a compound) in the middle, since this would also interfere with comprehension. The manuscript frequently divides words illogically at line-ends, and I have rejoined these without comment. The scribe clearly felt that line divisions should occasion no division in sense, and I have respected this belief. Standard abbreviations for 'and' and 'þæt' are expanded without mention, as are suspension marks representing 'm' and 'n'. The manuscript punctuation has been reproduced, even though it may sometimes be a little confusing. Generally speaking, points are used at the end of sentences, and usually at the end of clauses. Both high and low points are used, apparently without discrimination. Sometimes it is difficult to tell which is intended, but I have tried to reproduce them accurately, for the sake of those scholars who need information on such matters.

The numbering of the signs is taken over from Kluge's edition (see below) for ease of reference. However, I have not used his section numbering, or even his division into sections, since this does not correspond with paragraph divisions in the manuscript. Instead, I have reproduced the paragraphs into which the scribe divided the text, even though few of them represent coherent thematic sections. Sometimes they appear deliberately misleading, but they may nevertheless be of interest to readers, and even shed some light on the text. The opening initial of each manuscript paragraph is printed bold in this edition.

Previous Edition and Studies

The *Monasteriales Indicia* has already been edited by F. Kluge in *Techmers Internationale Zeitschrift für Allgemeine Sprachwissenschaft*, no. 2, for 1885. This edition contains few substantive errors, and even fewer that interfere with the understanding of the text, but it is not readily available to scholarship in English-speaking countries, as the *Internationale Zeitschrift* was clearly not as international as Techmer intended, and it ceased publication in 1890. Since then, a number of scholars have made contributions to the study of the text, which I have acknowledged in the Notes to the Edition and listed in the Bibliography. In 1989, David Sherlock, with whom I have discussed the text on numerous occasions, published a translation into modern English, a great advance as far as English-speaking readers are concerned. However, there is still a need for an accessible edition, taking into account the results of all work on the text to date, of this unique document for the history of English monasticism.

Title

The title *Monasteriales Indicia* comes from the Latin rubrics to the text in the manuscript, 'Incipiunt Monasteriales Indicia' and 'Expliciunt Monasteriales Indicia' (the beginning and the end of the monastic signs, respectively). Other scholars have emended this example of poor Anglo-Saxon latinity, but I have decided to retain it, not only in accordance with my general practice of preserving manuscript readings where they do not interfere with comprehension, but also because this unique denomination serves to differentiate the text here edited from all the others, mentioned above, which might be described as 'indicia monasterialia' (monastic signs).[15]

---

[15] For general works on monastic sign language, see Gougaud and van Rijnberk. In English, the best source of general information is Sherlock and Zajac's introduction to their edition, although Barakat's introduction to his book on modern Cistercian sign language is fuller.

MONASTERIALES

INDICIA

INCIPIUNT MONASTERIALES INDICIA·[1]

Þis sindon þa tacna þe mon[2] on mynstre[3] healdan sceal
þær mon[4] æfter regoles bebode swigan haldan wile and
geornlice mid godes fultume begyman sceal.

1. Ærest þæs abbudes tacen is þæt mon his twegen fingras to
   his heafde asette. and his feax mid genime·
2. Ðæs diacanes tacen is þæt mon mid hangiendre hande do
   swilce he gehwæde bellan cnyllan wille·
3. Gyf mon wæt be þam profoste tæcan wille[5] þonne rær þu
   þinne scytefinger ofer þin heafod forþi þæt is his tacen·
4. Ðonne is þæs horderes tacen þæt mon wrænce mid is
   hande swilce he wille loc hunlucan·
5. Ðæs magistres taccen is þe þa cild bewat þæt man set his
   twegen fingras on his twa eagan and hebbe up his litlan
   finger.
6. Ðæs cyricweardes tacen is þæt mon sette his twegen
   fingras on his twa eagan and do mid[6] his handa swylce he
   wille ane hangigende bellan· teon·
7. Gyf þu wæt be cyrcean tæcan wille þonne do þu mid
   þinum twan handum swylce þu bellan ringe· and sete þinne
   scytefinger to þinum muþe· and hine syððan up rær·

---

1 *this rubric is on folio 97 recto; the Old English heading follows on
the verso.*
2 *ms.* þemon
3 *ms.* mystre
4 þærmon *written twice, crossed out at end of line 1, retained at
beginning of line 2.*
5 *ms.* Gyf mon wille wæt be pam profoste tæcan wille
6 *ms.* domid

22

THE BEGINNING OF THE MONASTIC SIGNS.

These are the signs that are to be used in the monastery, and observed diligently with God's help, where it is desired to keep silence according to the command of the Rule.

1. First, the sign for the abbot is that one puts one's two fingers to one's head, and takes hold of one's hair with them.
2. The sign for the dean is that one makes as if one were ringing a small bell, with one's hand hanging down.
3. If it is intended to indicate something about the provost, then raise your index finger over your head, because that is his sign.
4. Then the sign for the cellarer is that one turns with one's hand as if one were unlocking a lock.
5. The sign for the master, who looks after the children, is that one puts one's two fingers to one's eyes, and holds up one's little finger.
6. The sign for the sacrist is that one puts one's two fingers to one's two eyes, and makes with one's hand, as if one were to pull a hanging bell.
7. If you want to indicate anything about the church, then make with your two hands as if you were ringing a bell, then put your index finger to your mouth, and then raise it up.

Ðis synd þara boca tacn þe mon on cyrican to god cundun þeowdome notigan sceal·

8. Ðonne þu antiphonariam habban wille þonne wege þu þine[7] swiþran hand· and crip þinne þuman forþon he is genotod·

9. Gif þu mæsse boc habban wille þonne wege þu þine hand do swilce þu bletsige.

10. Ðære pistol boce tacn ys þæt mon wecge his hand and wyrce crystelmæl on his heafde foran mid his þuman forþon þe mon ræt god spel þær on and eal swa on þære cristes bec.

11. Ðonne þu tropere haban wille þonne wege þu þine[8] swiran hand· and tyrn mid þinum swiþran scyte fingre ofer þine breost fore weard swilce þu notian wille·

12. Gyf þu hwilce lang wyrpe boc habban wille þonne strece[9] þu þine wynstran hand· and wege hi· and sete þine swyþran ofer þine wynstran earm be þære boce læncge·

13. Ðonne þu superumerale habban wille þonne stryc[10] þu of ufwerdum heafde mid þinum twam scyte fingran nyþerweard[11] forð for þine earmas· andlang þinra hleora·

14. Gyf þu halban habban wille þonne wege þu medemlice þin reaf mid þinre handa·

15. Donne þu gyrder habban wylle þonne sete þu þine handa fore wearde wiðneoþan þinne nafolan· and stric to þinum twam hyþum·

16. Ðonne þu stolan habban wille· do þu mid þinum twam handum on butan þinne sweoran· and stric siððan ofdune·

---

7 *ms.* þinne (*first* n *erased*).
8 'e' *over erasure.*
9 *ms.* srece
10 *ms.* sryc
11 98 *recto*

These are the signs for the books that are to be used in church at divine service.

8. When you want a gradual, then move your right hand and crook your thumb, because it is notated.

9. If you want a sacramentary, then move your hand and make as if you were giving a blessing.

10 The sign for the epistolary is that one moves one's hand and makes the sign of the cross on the front of one's head with one's thumb, because one reads the word of God in it, and likewise in the Gospels.

11. When you want a troper, then move your right hand and turn with your right index finger over your chest in front, as if you were notating.

12. If you want any rectangular book, then stretch your left hand, and move it about, and put your right over your left arm at the length of the book.

13. When you want a superhumeral, then stroke with your two index fingers from the top of your head downwards along your cheeks out towards your arms.

14. If you want an alb, then move your clothes slightly with your hand.

15. When you want a girdle, then put your hands in front of you below your navel and stroke to your two hips.

16. When you want a stole, put your two hands around your neck, and then stroke downwards.

17. Gyf þu mæssan[12] hacelan habban wille þonne stric þu mid tospræddum handum niþer ofer þine breost·

18. Ðonne þu handlin habban wille þonne stric þu mid þinre swyðran handa eclinga ofer þine wynstran·

19. Gyf þu offrunga habban wille þonne wege þu þin reaf·[13] and hefe up þine twa handa·

20. Ðæs calices tacn and ðæs disces is þæt man hebbe up his twa handa and bletsige·

21. Gyf þu oflætan habban wille þonne byg þu þinne scyte fynger to þinum þuman·

22. Ðonne þu win habban wille þonne do þu mid þinun twam fingrum. swilce þu tæppan of tunnan onteon wille·

23. Gyf þu winhorn habban wille þonne do þu mid þinum swiðran[14] scyte fingre on þine wynstran hand swilce þu tæppan teon wille· and rær up þinne scyte finger be þinum heofede·

24. Ðonne þu stor fæt habban wille þonne wend þu þine hand of dune and wege hi swilce þu styre·

25. Gyf þu taperas be þurfe þonne blaw þu on þinne scyte finger· and rær up þinne þuman·

26. Gyf þu candel· sticcan habban wille þonne blaw þu on þinum scyte fingre and hald þine hand sam locene swylce þu candel stæf hæbbe·

27. Gyf þe smælre candelle ge neodige þonne blaw þu on þinum scyte fingre·

28. Ðonne þu candel bryd habban wille astrehtre þinre winstran handa of sete hy eclinga mid þinre swiran.
Ðys syndan þara boca tacna þe mon æt uhtsange notian sceal.

---

[12] *ms.* þumæssan
[13] *ms.* wege þugþuþin reaf ('g' *erased*).
[14] 'ð' *added above line.*

17. If you want a mass vestment, then stroke with outspread hands down over your chest.
18. When you want a maniple, then stroke with your right hand on edge over your left.
19. If you want an offering-cloth, then move your clothes and lift up your two hands.
20. The sign for the chalice and paten is that one lifts up one's two hands and makes a blessing.
21. If you want the mass-bread, then bend your index finger to your thumb.
22. When you want wine, then make with your two fingers as if you were undoing the tap of a cask.
23. If you want a wine-flask, then make with your right index-finger on your left hand, as if you were pulling a tap, and raise up your index finger to your head.
24. When you want a censer, then turn your hand downwards and move it as if you were censing.
25. If you need tapers, then blow on your index finger and hold up your thumb.
26. If you want a candlestick, then blow on your index finger, and hold your hand half closed, as if you were holding a candlestick.
27. If you need a thin candle, then blow on your index finger.
28. When you want a candle board, with your left hand stretched out, press it edgeways with your right.
These are the signs for the books that are to be used at matins.

29. Gyf þu biblioðecan habban wille þonne wege þu þine hand and rær up þinne þuman and sete þine hand brad linge to þinum leore·[15]

30. Ðonne þe martirlogium geneodie þonne wege þu þine hand· and lege þinne swiðran scyte finger ofer þine hand· and lege þine hand bralinga to þinum hleore·

31. Gyf þu hwylce oþre boc habban wylle þe god spelles traht on sy þonne lege þu þine swyðran hand under þin hleor. and werc rode tacen on þin[16] heofod foran·

32. Ðonne þe salteres beþurfe þonne stric þu mid þinum swyðran scyte finger on þine[17] wynstran hand swilce þu micel bewytan wille·

33. Hymneres tacen is þæt mon wæcge bradlinga his hand and rære up his litlan finger·

34. Ðonne þu leoht fæt abban wylle tospræddum fingre rær up þine swiðran hand and pyf on þinne scyte finger·

35. Ðonne þu micelan rode abban wylle þonne lege þu þinne finger· ofer þinne swyðran finger and rær up þinne þuman.

36. Litelere rode tacen is ealswa rær up þonne litlan finger·

37. Ðonne þu on ænigre stowe gewædne candel sticcan abban wille· þonne do þu swa we ær beforan cwædon· and rær up þinne litlan finger·

38. Gyf þu inne cyricean sittan wille for wylcere untrumnysse· þonne wende he his hand adune· and ahnigenum heafede him leafe biddan and his hand on breost[18] asette·

39. Gyf þu wille þæt hwa sittendra manna up[19] arise þonne wend þu þine hand and hi be dæle up abræd·

---

15 *98 verso*

16 *ms.* onþin

17 *ms.* onþine

18 *ms.* onbreost

19 *ms.* 'a' *erased between* manna *and* up.

29. If you want a bible, then move your hand about and hold up your thumb and put your hand flat against your cheek.

30. When you need a legendary, then move your hand and lay your right index finger over your hand and lay your hand flat against your cheek.

31. If you want any other book in which there is a gospel text, then lay your right hand under your cheek and make the sign of the cross in front of your head.

32. When you require a psalter, then stroke with your right index finger on your left hand, as if you were paying great attention.

33. The sign for a hymnal is that one moves one's hand sideways and holds up one's little finger.

34. When you want a lamp, lift up your right hand with outspread fingers and blow on your index finger.

35. When you want a large cross, then lay your finger over your right finger and hold up your thumb.

36. The sign for a small cross is just the same; raise the little finger.

37. When in any place you need a small candlestick, then do as we said before and raise your little finger.

38. If you want to sit down in church on account of any infirmity, then let him turn his hand downwards and ask permission with bowed head and put his hand to his chest.

39. If you want anyone who is sitting down to stand up, then turn your hand and open it out upwards a little.

40. Gyf þu wylle þæt he sytte þonne wend þu adune· and hi bedæle adune læt·

41. Gyf man hwylcum breþer byt hwæt on ufan þæt he genoh[20] hæbbe þonne wend þu his hand bradlinga adune· and astrehtre hwonlice hy styrige·

42. Gyf he þæt ge bodene habban wille þonne wende he his hand eclinga adune and wonlice wið his wyrd styrige·

43. Gyf he hyt nelle he hwonlice eac framweard styrige·

44. Gyf þu hwæt be capitel huse tæcan wylle þonne sete þu þine hand on þin heafod foran and hwon hniwa swilce þu þe for gyfenesse bidde·

45. Ðonne þu gehwædne martirlogium habban wille þonne wege þu þine hand· and lege þinne scyte finger ofer þine þrotan and rær up þinne litlan finger·

46. Regoles tacen is þæt þu wecge þine hand and stryce mid þinum scyte fyngre andlang þinre wynstran handa swylce[21] þu regolige.

47. Gyf þu gyrde habban wille þonne wege þine fyst swylce þu swingan[22] wille·

48. Ðonne þu swype habban wille þonne wege þu þine fyst swa swa we beforan cwædon and rær up þine twæg fingras·

49. Gyf þu hwæt be beoddernes[23] tacne tæcan wylle þonne sete þu þine þry fingras swilce ðu mete to muðe do.

50. Donne þu setrægel habban wille þonne plice þu ðine agene geweda mid twam fingrum to spred þine twa handa· and gewe hi swylce þu setl gesydian wille·

---

20 *ms.* hegenoh
21 *99 recto*
22 *ms.* swigan
23 *ms.* bebeoddernes

40. If you want him to sit down, turn (it) downwards and let it move down a little.
41. If any brother is offered more of anything, of which he has enough, then turn his hand downwards, in a horizontal position, and move it about slightly, spread out.
42. If he wants what is offered, then let him turn his hand downwards on edge and move it somewhat towards him .
43. If he does not want it, let him also move (it) slightly away.
44. If you want to indicate something about the chapter house, then put your hand on the front of your head and bow a little as if you were asking forgiveness.
45. When you want a small martyrology, then move your hand and lay your index finger over your throat, and raise your little finger.
46. The sign for the Rule is that you move your hand and stroke with your index finger along your left hand, as if you were ruling.
47. If you want a rod, then move your fist as if you were going to hit (someone).
48. When you want a scourge, then move your fist as we said before, and raise your two fingers.
49. If you want to indicate anything by the sign for the refectory, then place your three fingers as if you were putting food into your mouth.
50. When you want a seat cover, then pinch your own clothes with two fingers, spread out your two hands, and move them as if you were arranging a seat.

51. Gyf þu meterædere fyld stol habban wille oþþe oþrum men· þonne clæm þu þine handa togædere· and wege[24] hi þam gemete þe þu dest[25] þonne þu hine fyldan[26] wylt·

52. Gyf þu sceat habban wille oððe wapan[27] þonne sete þu þine twa handa ofer þinum bearme and to bræd hi swillce sceat astrecce·

53. Gyf þe disces beþurfe· þonne hefe þu up þine oþre hand and tospræd þine fingras·

54. Ðonne[28] þu laf habban wylle þonne sete þu þine twegen þuman to gædere and þine twegen scyte fingras æðerne foran ongean· oþerne·

55. Gyf þe syxes genyodige[29] þonne snid þu mid þinum fingre ofer þonne oþerne swylce þu cyrfan wille·

56. Gyf þu sticcan be hofige þonne wege þu þine hand swilce þu mid sticcan etan wille·

57. Gesodenra wyrta tacen is þæt þu do mid þinre oðre handa nyþer weard be þære[30] sidan swylce þu wyrta scearffian wille·

58. Ðonne þu grene wyrta habban wille þonne sete þu þinne finger on þine[31] wenstran hande·

59. Gyf þe læces lyste þonne do þu mid þinum fingre swilce þu borige inn on[32] þine hand· and do bralinga þine hand to þinre nasan swilce þu hwæt gestince·

---

[24] *ms.* gege
[25] *ms.* þudest
[26] 'a' *added above line between* y *and* l.
[27] *ms.* papan
[28] *Initial missing in ms.*
[29] 'ge' *added above line.*
[30] *ms.* beþære
[31] *ms.* onþine
[32] *ms.* innon

51. If you want a folding stool for the mealtime reader or anyone else, then clasp your hands together and move them in the way that you do when you want to fold it.
52. If you want a cloth or a napkin, then put your two hands over your lap, and spread them as if you were smoothing out a cloth.
53. If you need a dish, then lift up your other hand, and spread your fingers.
54. When you want bread, then put your two thumbs together, and your two index fingers one against the other in front.
55. If you need a knife, then cut with your finger over the other, as if you were slicing.
56. If you require a skewer, then move your hand as if you were eating with a skewer.
57. The sign for boiled vegetables is that you move your other hand downwards by the side, as if you were shredding vegetables.
58. If you want raw vegetables, then put your finger on your left hand.
59. If you would like leeks, then make with your finger as if you were boring into your hand, and put your hand flat to your nose as if you were smelling something.

60. Briwes tacan is þæt þu wecge þine fyst swilce þu briw·
hrere·

61. Ðonne[33] þu pipor habban wille þonne cwoca þu mid þinum
scyte[34] finger ofer oþerne·

62. Gyf þu beana habban wille þonne sete þu þinne scyte
finger fore weardne on þines þuman forman[35] liðe·

63. Pesena[36] tacen is þæt mon sette his[37] þuman on his litlan
finger fore weardne·

64. Ðonne þu cyse habban wille sete þonne þine twa handa to
gædere bralinga swilce þu wringan wille·

65. Gyf þu buteran[38] habban wylle oððe smeoru þonne stric þu
mid þrim fingrum on þine inne wearde hand·

66. Gyf þe meolce lyste þonne strocca þu þinne wynstra finger
mid þinre swyþran hande þam gelice swylce þu melce·

67. Gyf þu ægera be þurfe þonne scrapa þu mid þinum fingre
up on þinne wynstran þuman·

68. Ðonne þu scealt habban wylle þonne geþeoddum þinum
þrim fingrum hryse þine hand swylce þu· hwæt seltan
wylle·

69. Huniges tacen is þæt þu sette þinne finger on þine tungan·

70. Ðonne þu fisc habban wylle þonne. wege þu þyne hand
þam gemete þe he deþ his tægl þonne he swymð·

71. Æles tacen is þæt mon wecge his swyþran hand and sette
syþþan ofer his wynstran earm· and a strehtre his wynstran
hande strice þwyrs ofer mid þære swyþran· swylce he hine

---

33 *Initial missing.*
34 *Written over erasure.*
35 *ms.* for man
36 *ms.* Cesena
37 *Written over erasure.*
38 *99 verso*

60. The sign for pottage is that you move your fist as if you were stirring pottage.
61. When you want pepper, then knock with one index finger on the other.
62. If you want beans, then put your index finger forward on the first joint of your thumb.
63. The sign for peas is that one puts one's thumb on the front of one's little finger.
64. When you want cheese, then put your two hands together flat, as if you were pressing (it).
65. If you want butter or fat, then stroke with three fingers on the inside of your hand.
66. If you would like milk, then stroke your left finger with your right hand in the way in which you milk.
67. If you need eggs, then scrape with your finger up your left thumb.
68. When you want salt, then shake your hand with your three fingers together, as if you were salting something.
69. The sign for honey is that you place your finger on your tongue.
70. If you want fish, then move your hand in the way that it moves its tail when it swims.
71. The sign for eel is that one moves one's right hand, and then puts it on one's left arm, with the left hand stretched out, and strokes across it with one's right hand, as if one

corflige swa swa mon æl deð þonne hine mon· on spite[39]
stagan wyle·

72. Gif þu ostran habban wylle þonne clæm þu þinne wynstran
hand ðam gemete þe þu ostran on handa hæbbe and do
mid sexe oððe mid fingre swylce þu ostran scenan wylle·

73. Ðonne þe æpples lyste þonne cryp þu þinne swiþran
þuman to midde wearde þinre handa and befoh hine mid
þinum fingre and rær up þine fæste·

74. Gyf þu peran wille þonne do þu ymbe þine fyste swa we
nu wið foran cwædon and geþeod siðþan þine· fingras
tosomne forð hand lenge.

75. Ðonne þu plyman habban wille þonne clæm þu eal
begelicum þine wynstran hand and stric mid þinum scyte
fingre anlang þinre[40] fyste·

76. Cyrsena tac is þæt þu sette þinne winstran þuman on þines
lytlan fingres lið and twenge hine siððan mid þara swiþran
hande

77. Gyf þe slana lyste þonne sete þu eall swa þinne þuman and
pyt mid þinum scyte fingre in þine wynstran[41] hand on
þornes getacnunge þe hi on weaxað·

78. Ðonne þu for hwylcere neode sealt flæsc wille þonne
twenge þu mid þinre swiðran neoþe wearde þine wynstran
þær se lyra þiccost si· and do mid þinum þrim fingrum
swilcce þu[42] sealte.[43]

79. Ðonne þu cuppan oððe iustitian wylle þonne do þu þine
hand. nyþerweard· and to bræd þine fingras·

---

[39] *ms.* onswite

[40] *ms.* þire

[41] *ms.* swynstran (*expecting* swyþran).

[42] *ms.* þe

[43] *100 recto*

were cutting it, just as one does to eels when one wants to stick them on a spit.

72. If you want an oyster, then close your left hand, as if you had an oyster in your hand, and make with a knife or with your fingers as if you were going to open the oyster.

73. When you wish for an apple, then crook your right thumb into the middle of your hand and take hold of it with your fingers and lift up your fist.

74. If you want a pear, then do with your fist as we have just said and join your fingers together out to the length of your hand.

75. When you want plums, then clasp your left hand in the same way, and stroke with your index finger along your fist.

76. The sign for cherries is that you put your left thumb on the joint of your little finger, and then pinch it with the right hand.

77. If you want sloes, then put your thumb the same way and poke with your index finger into your left hand as a sign of the thorn that they grow on.

78. If you want salt meat for any reason, then pinch with your right (hand) low down on your left, where the flesh is thickest, and make with your three fingers as if you were salting.

79. When you want a cup or a measure, then put your hand down low and spread out your fingers.

80. Ðonne þu hlid. habban wylle þonne hafa þu þine wynstran hand[44] sam locene· and eac swa swa þa swyþran· and hwylf hy syþþan ofer þa wynstran eal swylce þu cuppan hlide.

81. Micelre[45] blede tacen is þæt þu arære up þine swyþran hand· and to spræd þine fingras· and lege syþan[46] þinne scyte finger to þinum wælerum· and rær up þinne þuman·

82. Gyf þu lytel drence fæt habban· wylle þonne rær þu up þine þry fingras· and lege þinne swyþran scyte finger to þinum wælerum· and rær up þinne lytlan finger·

83. Ðonne þu drincan wylle þonne lege þu þinne scete finger and lang þines muþes·

84. Gyf þe ge dryptes wines lyste· þonne do þu mid þinum swyþran scyte fingre on þine wynstran· hand swylce þu tæppian wille· and wænd þinne scyte finger adune· and twængc hine mid þinum twam fingrum swylce þu of sumne dropan strican wylle.

85. Beores tacen is þæt þu gnide þine hand on þa[47] oþre·

86. Ðonne þu wyrtdrenc[48] haban wille þonne wege þu þine fyst[49] swilce þu wyrta cnocian wille· and lege[50] þinne scyte finger to þinum welerum·

87. Gyf þu hwæt be slæpernes tacne tæccean wylle þonne lyge þu þinne swyþran hand under þin swyþre hleor·

88. Ðonne þu blacernes behofige· þonne tern þu[51] mid þinum scete fingre on earþan butan þu elles wite on hwæt·[52] and

---

[44] *possibly an erased letter after* 'd'.
[45] *ms.* Wicelre
[46] *ms.* swyþan (*expecting* swyþran *again* - 'w' *over erasure*)
[47] *ms.* onþa
[48] *ms.* þuburhreste
[49] *above line, words below erased.*
[50] *ms.* andlege
[51] *ms.* ternþu
[52] *ms.* onhwæt

80. When you want a lid, then lift up your left hand half closed and likewise the right, and then curve it over the left, just as if you were putting the lid on a cup.
81. The sign for a large bowl is that you lift up your right hand and spread out your fingers, and then lay your index finger on your lips and raise your thumb.
82. If you want a little drinking vessel, then raise your three fingers, and lay your right index finger to your lips and lift up your little finger.
83. When you want to drink, then lay your index finger along your mouth.
84. If you wish for dripped wine, then make with your right index finger on your left hand as if you were tapping (a cask), and turn your index finger downwards and pinch it with your two fingers as if you wanted to wipe off a drop.
85. The sign for 'beer' is that you grind your hand on the other.
86. When you want a herbal drink then move your fist as if you were crushing herbs, and lay your index finger on your lips.
87. If you want to indicate something by the sign for the dormitory, then lay your right hand under your right cheek.
88. When you require a lamp, then circle with your index finger on the earth, unless you know on what else, and

wæt mid þinum scyte fingre on midden swylce þu weocan settan wylle·

89. Ðonne þu bed reaf habban wylle þonne wege þu þin reaf and lege þine hand to þinum hleore.

90. Pyles[53] tacen is þæt þu mid þinum scyte fingre sume feþer tacnum ge strice on þyne wynstran hand inne wearde· and lecge to þinum earon·

91. Gyf þu swyftleras[54] habban wylle· þonne sete þu þinne scyte finger uppon þinne fot· and stric on twa[55] healfa þines fet þam gemete þe hi gesceapene[56] beoð·

92. Socca tacen is þæt þu sette þinne scyte finger· and rær up þinne þuman·

93. Ðonne is þara sceona tacen þæt þu sette forð rihte· þinne scete finger uppon þinne fot butan oðre becnunge[57]

94. [.]yna[58] tunes tacen is þæt þu sette þinne swyþran hand brad linga ofer þinne innoð· and þu be þam[59] tacne þe leafe scealt æt þinum ealdre abyddan gyf þe þyder lyst·

95. Gyf þu hwat be bæðernes[60] tacne tæcan wille þonne stric þu mid þinre swiðran hande bralinga ofer þine breost· and ofer þinne innoð swilce þu þe þwean wille.

96. Ðonne þu þe be tacnunga[61] biddan wille þæt þu þin heafod þwean mote þonne stric þu mid bradre hande on þin[62] feax swilce þu hit þwea·

---

53 *initial omitted in ms.*
54 *ms.* swyft leras
55 *ms.* ontwa
56 *ms.* gesceawene
57 *100 verso*
58 *initial omitted.*
59 *ms.* þubeþam
60 *ms.* bebæðernes
61 *ms.* tancnunga
62 *ms.* onþin

wet with your index finger in the middle, as if you were going to set a wick.

89. When you want a bedcover, then move your clothes and lay your hand to your cheek.

90. The sign for a pillow is that you stroke the sign of a feather inside your left hand with your index finger, and lay it to your ear.

91. If you want slippers, then put your index finger on your foot and stroke the two sides of your foot, in the way in which they are made.

92. The sign for 'socks' is that you place your index finger (as above) and raise your thumb.

93. Then the sign for shoes is that you place your index finger straight on your foot without any other indication.

94. The sign for the privy is that you put your right hand flat over your belly and by this sign you must ask permission of your superior, if you want to go there.

95. If you want to indicate something by the sign for the bath-house, then stroke with your right hand flat over your chest and your belly, as if you were washing.

96. When you want to request in sign language that you may wash your head, then stroke with your flat hand on your hair, as if you were washing it.

97. Gyf þe wæteres geneodige þonne do þu swylce þu þine handa þwean wille.

98. Ðonne þu sapan abban wille þonne gnid þu þinne handa to gædere

99. Nægel sexes tacn[63] his þæt þu mid þinum scite fingre do ofer þinne oþerne swilce þu ceorfan wille and straca syþþan on þin[64] leor mid þinum fingre swilce þu scearan wille·

100. Ðonne þu camb· habban wylle þonne stric þu mid þinum fingrum on þin feax nyþer weard swilce þu cembe þe·

101. Gyf þu hemeþe habban wille þonne nim þu[65] slyfan þe on hand[66] and wege hi·

102. Brecena tacen[67] is þæt þu strice mid þinum twam handam up on þin[68] þeah.

103. Ðonne þu wynyngas habban wille þonne do þu mid þinum twam handum on butan þine sceancan·

104. Gyf þu hosa habban wille þonne stric þu upweard[69] on þinum[70] sceancum mid þinum twam handum·

105. Pylecan[71] tacen his þæt þu strece forð þin wenstre hand stoc· and plyce innan mid þinre wynstran hande·

106. Ðonne þu cuglan habban wylle þonne wege þu þinne earmellan· and foh to þinum hode·

---

[63] *ms.* tanc
[64] *ms.* onþin
[65] *ms.* nimþu
[66] *ms.* onhand
[67] *ms.* tancen
[68] *ms.* onþin
[69] *ms.* uppe ard
[70] *ms.* onþinum
[71] *ms.* Gylecan

97. If you need water, then make as if you were going to wash your hands.
98. When you want soap, then rub your hands together.
99. The sign for a nail-knife is that you make with your index finger on your other as if you were cutting, and then stroke with your finger on your cheek as if you were shaving.
100. When you want a comb, then stroke downwards on your hair with your fingers, as if you were combing it.
101. If you want a shirt, take your sleeve in your hand and move it.
102. The sign for underpants is that you stroke with your two hands up your thigh.
103. When you want leg bands, then make with your two hands around your shin (as if you were putting them on).
104. If you want stockings, then stroke upwards on your shin with your two hands.
105. The sign for a pelisse is that you stretch out your left cuff and pluck inside it with your left hand.
106. When you want a cowl, then move your sleeve and take hold of your hood.

107. Gyf þu to hwilcere gehirsumnesse scapulares· beþurfe þonne stric þu eclinga mid ægðere hande ofer æðerne earm ymbe þæt utan þe þæs scapularæs hand stoca ateoriað·

108. Ðonne þu glofan abban wille þonne stric þu þa oþre hand mid þære oþre bralinga·

109. Sceara tacen[72] is þæt þu wecge þinne scyte finger and þone midemistan on þinre[73] swiðran hande to somum claðe swilce þu hine mid scearan ceorfan wille oððe ymb þin heafod swilce þu efysian wille·

110. Gyf þe nædle beþurfe þonne feald þu mid þinre swiðran hande þane hem þines wynstran earm stoces ofer þinne wynstran scyte finger[74] and do þær ofer mid þrim fingrum swilce þu seowian wille.

111. Ðæs bæcernes tacne is þæt mon mid bam sam locone handum to gædere swilce þu dah brædan wille·

112. Ðonne þu græf habban wille· þonne sete þu þine þri fingras tosomne swilce þu græf hæbbe and styra þine fingras swilce þu write· and bycna syþþan mid þinum scyte fingre·

113. Gyf þu gehwæde wæxbreda habban wille þonne strece þu þine twa handa and sete[75] hy neoþan tosomne and feald to gædere swilce þu weax breda fealde·

114. Ðonne þu micel weax bred habban wille þonne stric þu mid þinum twam fingrum on þine breost fore wearde swilce þu dylige and stryce þinne earm and sete þine hand on þines wynstran earmes byge·

---

72 *ms.* tancen
73 *ms.* onþinre
74 *101 recto*
75 *ms.* and sete *twice, crossed out second time.*

107. If you need a scapular for any duty, then stroke with both hands on edge over both arms around the outside where the cuffs of the scapular finish.

108. When you want gloves, then stroke one hand with the other flat.

109. The sign for scissors is that you move your index finger and the middle one on your right hand on some cloth, as if you were going to cut it with scissors, or around your head, as if you were going to cut your hair.

110. If you need a needle, then fold the hem of your left sleeve over your left index finger with your right hand, and do over it with your three fingers as if you were sewing.

111. The sign for the bake house is that you (make) with both half-closed hands together, as if you were pulling out dough.

112. When you want a stylus, then put your three fingers together, as if you were holding a stylus, and move your fingers as if you were writing, and point with your index finger.

113. If you want small wax tablets, then stretch out your two hands and place them together at the bottom and fold them together as if you were folding tablets.

114. When you want a large tablet, then stroke with your two fingers in front of your chest, as if you were erasing, and stroke your arm, and put your hand on the elbow of your left arm.

115. Gyf þu reogol sticcan næbbe þonne strece þu þine hand up weard and stric mid þinum scyte fingre andlang þinre wynstran hande swilce þu regolige·

116. Ðonne þu blec horn habban wille þonne hafa þu þine þri fingras[76] swilce þu dypan wille and awend þine hand adune and clyce þine fingras swilce þu blæc horn niman wille

117. Fiþere tacen is þæt þu geþeode þine þri fingras[77] tosomne swilce þu feþere hæbe and hi dype[78] and styre þine fingras swilce þu writan[79] wille·

118. Ðæs cyninges tacen is þæt þu wende þine hand adune and be foh þine heofod ufeweard eallum fingrum on cynhelmes tacne.

119. Cyninges wifes tacen is þæt þu strece onbutan heofod and sete syððan þine hand bufon þin heofod·

120. Bisceopes[80] tacen is þæt þu strice mid þinre hande ofer æðere eaxle niþerweard ofer þine breost on rode tacne·

121. Gyf þu hwæt be wylcum[81] munece tæcan wille þe þu his tacen ne cunne þonne nim þu þe be þinum hode·

122. Mynecena tacen is þæt þu sette þine twegen scyte fingras on þin heofod· foran and strice siþþan adune andlang þinra hleora on þæs halig ryftes tacnunge.

123. Gyf þu mæsse preost habban wille þe munuc ne sy þonne stric þu mid þinum scyte fingre swilce þu trændel wyrce

---

[76] *ms.* þrifingras
[77] *ms.* þrifingras
[78] *ms.* hidype
[79] *ms.* wirtan
[80] *ms.* Ðisceopes
[81] *ms.* bewylcum

115. If you have no ruler, then stretch your hand up and stroke with your index finger along your left hand as if you were ruling.

116. When you want an ink-well, then lift up your three fingers as if you were going to dip (a pen), and turn your hand down and close your fingers as if you were going to pick up an ink-well.

117. The sign for a quill is that you join your three fingers together as if you were holding a quill, and dip them, and move your fingers as if you were going to write.

118. The sign for the king is that you turn your hand downwards and hold the top of your head with all your fingers in the sign of a crown.

119. The sign for the king's wife is that you stroke round your head, and then put your hand on top of your head.

120. The sign for the bishop is that you stroke with your hand over each shoulder down over your chest in the sign of the cross.

121. If you want to indicate anything about any monk whose sign you do not know, then take hold of yourself by the hood.

122. The sign for nuns is that you put your two index fingers on the front of your head and stroke down along your cheeks in the sign of the veil.

123. If you want a priest who is not a monk, then stroke with your index finger, as if you were making a circle, and

and astrehtre þinre hande on þam gemete[82] swilce þu bletsige·

124. Ðonne þu diacon abban wille þonne stric þu ealgelice mid þinum scyte fingre and wyrc cristes mæl on þin heafod foran on þæs[83] halgan godspelles getacnunge·

125. Be mædennnes hades preostes tacen is þæt þu strice swa we wið foran cwædon on þin hleor mid þine scyte fingre·

126. Lædes mannes tacen is þæt þu ðe[84] mid ealre hande be þinum cynne nime[85] swilce þu þe[86] be bearde[87] niman wille·

127. Gewylces ungehadodes[88] wifes tacen is[89] þæt þu mid fore weardum fingrum þin fore wearde heafod fram þam anum earan to þon oþrum on bindan tacne·

Ex pliciunt monasteriales indicia·

---

[82] *101 verso*
[83] *ms.* onþæs
[84] *ms.* þuðe
[85] *ms.* nyme nime
[86] *ms.* þuþe
[87] *ms.* bebearde
[88] *ms.* unge ha dodes
[89] *ms.* tacenis

with your outstretched hand in the manner in which you give a blessing.

124. When you want a deacon, then stroke with your index finger just the same, and make the sign of the cross on the front of your head in indication of the holy gospel.

125. The sign for a celibate priest is that you stroke on your cheek with your index finger as we said before.

126. The sign for a layman is that you take hold of your chin with your whole hand, as if you were taking yourself by the beard.

127. The sign for any woman not in orders is that you (stroke) with the tip of your finger on the front of your head from one ear to the other in the sign of a (head) band.

The end of the monastic signs.

ii. Diacan

iiii. hnorðerne

u. magiſtre

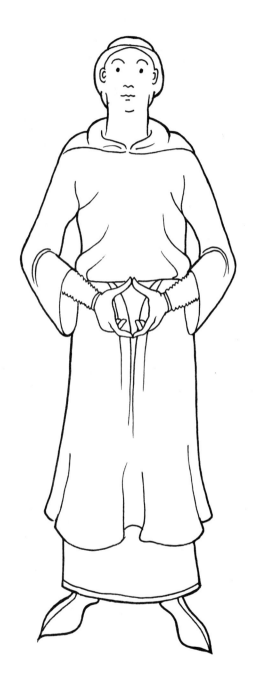

liu. laf

cxxuii. pif

NOTES ON THE

MONASTIC SIGNS

NOTES ON THE MONASTIC SIGNS

1. This is not a pulling of the forelock, but more like a salute, as the Cluny list (sign 70, for 'rule', which is indicated by the sign for 'abbot' because St Benedict was an abbot) explains: 'ut capillum super aurem pendentem cum duobus digitis aprehendas' (that you take hold of the hair hanging over the ear with two fingers). This suggests that monastic haircuts, apart from the tonsure, were not terribly short.

2. This is the same as the Cluny sign for 'prior' (no. 85) 'simula cum duobus digitis scillam tenere et ita eam sonare' (pretend to hold a little bell with two fingers and so ring it). Evidently the official called 'diacan' in England performed the functions of the continental, and later English, prior, who was in charge of the monastery under the abbot. In monasteries attached to cathedrals, such as Christ Church, the prior was the effective head of the house, since the titular head was the bishop or archbishop. In the *Regularis Concordia*, the dean (decanus) is next in seniority after the abbot and provost (see next sign), although neither of these officials is mentioned frequently, while 'prior' is used to mean 'senior' generally, sometimes meaning the abbot himself, sometimes a miscellaneous monastic official.[1]

3. This sign appears to be related to William of Hirsau's sign (254) for 'prepositus' (provost; the Cluny list has no such sign): 'fac indicem prominere in fronte' (make your index finger stick out on your forehead), which, as William explains 'est signum bovi, eo quod ipse sit talium provisor' (is the sign of the ox, because he is the provider of such things). In the Cluniac order, the provost was an administrative officer who dealt with the day to day running of the monastery and its estates.[2] In the

---

[1] *Concordia*, chapter 4, paragraphs 41 and 57, and, for 'prior', *passim*; also pp. xxx-xxxi of Dom Thomas Symons' introduction to the text.

[2] Evans, p. 67.

Concordia he is intermediate in status between the abbot and the dean, but his duties are not explained (see no. 2, above).
4. The same as the Cluny sign for 'cellararius' (no. 89).
5. Similar to the Cluny sign for 'magister puerorum' (no. 97), except that the Cluny sign for looking (after) uses only one finger and one eye: 'digitum pollici proximum pone subtus oculum' (put the finger next to the thumb underneath the eye). The little finger is the sign for 'small' in all lists, even where it is not explained as such (see Cluny no. 86, where it is made explicit).
6. The Cluny sign for 'custos ecclesiae' (no. 87) mimes ringing the bell, but does not use the 'looking' sign.
7. This is unlike the sign for 'church' in any other list, many of which, surprisingly, have none at all. David Sherlock suggests the raising of the index finger may indicate singing or praying. Alternatively, it could mean the silence to be observed in the church except during these activities.
8. Helmut Gneuss's study of Anglo-Saxon liturgical books, which looks at the surviving manuscripts, as well as vocabulary, shows that this book is what is now known as a gradual, containing all the sung portions of the mass, both proper and ordinary, not just the antiphons. The description of this sign is a little obscure, but it is explained by the following Cluny signs: the general sign for a book (no. 64), 'extende manum et move, sicut folium libri moveri solet' (stretch out the hand and move it, as the page of a book is normally moved), and the sign for 'antiphonarius' (no. 69) 'ut pollicem inflexas propter neumas, que sunt ita inflexe' (that you bend your thumb on account of the neums, which are bent like that). Neums are the medieval musical notes, many of them hook-shaped, which preceded the current system of notation.

That 'notian', here and in sign 11, means 'provide with musical notation' was suggested by Schlutter in 1922, in an article criticizing the first edition of the New (Oxford) English Dictionary; the Dictionary gave no examples of this meaning before 1440. This would be a Latin loan-word, unique to this text, a homonym of the native 'notian' meaning 'use, fulfil' (which occurs in the heading immediately before this sign). The second edition of NED (1989) has no instance of a musical 'note' in English before c.1300, and none of 'noted' in this sense before the 19th century (although, strangely, both the passages quoted relate to antiphonaries).

9. According to Gneuss, this is a sacramentary, containing not the complete text of the mass, but only the prayers said by the celebrant, and the proper texts. This identification had already been made by Karl Christ. The Cluny sign for 'missale' (no. 65) adds to the general sign for 'book', 'ut facias signum crucis', presumably the same as the sign here.

10. Gneuss regards 'pistolboc' as meaning the epistolary, a lectionary including not only the epistles but also passages from Acts, the Apocalypse and the Old Testament, which are sometimes read in place of the epistle, although no such book survives from Anglo-Saxon England. 'Cristes boc' he explains as probably a complete Gospel book with lections marked in it, rather than just a gospel lectionary. Cluny has separate signs for 'textus evangelii' (no. 66) and 'liber epistolaris' (no. 67). In the first, the sign of the cross is made on the forehead, as here, but in the second it is made on the chest. None of the continental lists mentions using the thumb, but this is specified in both Bury lists and the list from Syon (Jarecki no. 13, Sherlock and Zajac 24; Aungier p. 407, l. 14), and appears therefore to be an English feature.

11. A troper is the book containing musical interpolations into the chant of the mass. None of the continental lists have this sign, or one like it. The Bury St Edmunds lists have a sign for 'troponarius' (Jarecki no. 39, Sherlock and Zajac 52), based on their sign for 'sequentia' (sequences were also musical interpolations), but this is different both from the Cluny sign for sequence (no. 62) and from the Old English sign for troper. This sign is therefore unique to the *Indicia*, possibly based on a

misunderstanding, but possibly on a genuine difference in usage. For 'notian', see no. 8, above.

12. Presumably a book longer in format than the usual squarish proportions. Christ states that both long and wide formats existed side by side in the early Middle Ages. Cluny has a different sign for 'long' (no. 63) 'trahe manum per ventrem de deorsum' (draw the hand over the belly from below), which is also found in the other continental lists, while in the two Bury lists, length is indicated by drawing the hand across from the left shoulder to the right (sign 19 in Jarecki, 33 in Sherlock and Zajac). No other list has a sign for 'rectangular', or for identifying a book by its shape.

13. William of Hirsau has a sign for 'humerale' (no. 181; not in Cluny), in which 'manus ex utraque parte capitis equaliter positas deorsum trahas' (you move your hands, placed equally on either side of your head, downwards). According to a recent study of ecclesiastical dress, '(super)humerale' means the amice, a neck-cloth which is put on the head like a hood, before the other vestments, then rolled down over their necklines like a collar.[3] The sign in William and the *Indicia* could represent this action, if not very clearly.

14. The alb is a long white tunic worn by the officiating priest, and some other participants, at mass. This sign appears to be incomplete, since taking hold of one's garment is a general sign for 'clothing' (see below, e.g. no. 89). Cluny has no sign for 'alb' but William (no. 182) directs one to take hold of the garment on the chest and move it downwards. Such an instruction could have been omitted from the *Indicia*, as could the action prescribed in the Bury lists (no. 6 in Jarecki, 5 in Sherlock and Zajac), in which the hands are moved down the opposite arms one after the other.

15. Presumably the girdle worn with the alb. This has no sign in the continental lists, although they have a related sign for the

---

[3] Mayo, pp. 132-3.

belt worn with the shirt as part of the regular habit (Cluny no. 49), in which the hands are moved from the sides to the middle, in the opposite direction to this sign. The Bury lists, however, have a sign used for both liturgical and everyday girdles (no. 58 in Jarecki, 8 and 183 in Sherlock and Zajac), in which the hands move outwards from the navel, as in the *Indicia*. This appears therefore to be an English feature, rather than representing a difference in the way liturgical girdles and ordinary belts were worn or fastened.

16. The continental lists have no sign for the stole, a long strip of material worn round the neck and hanging down in front, but both Bury lists have a sign (Jarecki no. 7, Sherlock and Zajac 6) in which both index fingers are moved downwards from the shoulders to the waist. This is clearly related to the *Indicia*'s sign, although not the same. When worn under the chasuble (see no. 17), the stole is supposed to be crossed over the chest and secured by the girdle, but these signs seem to suggest it hanging loosely on either side. A tenth-century stole is among the objects found in St Cuthbert's coffin in Durham.[4]

17. This is presumably the chasuble (casula), the uppermost of the garments worn by the celebrant at mass, at this period a tent-like garment with a hole in the middle for the head. The signs for 'casula' in both William of Hirsau (no. 180; not in Cluny) and the Bury lists (Jarecki no. 5, Sherlock and Zajac 4), involve pretending to put it on, with the sign of the cross in William for its liturgical use. William's description of this, 'utraque manu simula te eam tenere et sic quasi ad induendum movere' (pretend that you are taking hold of it with both hands and so moving them as if to put it on) suggests that the *Indicia* could intend the same action, even though it does not explain what it represents.

18. 'Handlin' translates the literal meaning of 'manipulus', 'hand-towel', but in liturgical use this became a strip of fabric

---

[4] see Battiscombe.

hanging over the left wrist. The Bury signs indicate this more clearly than does the *Indicia*: 'simula in sinistro brachio illum pendere et quasi sub brachio dextra manu illum apprehendens' (pretend to hang it on the left arm and as if taking hold of it beneath the arm with the right hand - Jarecki no. 8, Sherlock and Zajac 7). The maniple was often considered as a companion piece to the stole, and St Cuthbert's treasure contains a tenth-century maniple, as well as a stole (see no. 16 above). No continental list has a sign for 'maniple'. The *Indicia*'s signs for vestments (nos 13-18) are given in the order in which the priest would put them on.

19. Since it begins with moving the garment, this sign must mean some kind of vestment or cloth, probably the corporal, on which the chalice and the host stand on the altar.[5] Perhaps something is missing from the headword 'offrung', which alone would suggest either the host itself (see sign 21) or its formal elevation. William of Hirsau has a sign for 'pannum ad offerendum aptatum' (cloth suitable for making an offering - no. 161) which consists of a sign for cloth and one for offering, but both signs are different from those in the *Indicia*, that for cloth simulating weaving, and for the offering, 'addita in superficie manus deosculatione' (with a kiss on the top surface of the hand added). The Bury and Syon lists have a sign (Jarecki no. 4, Sherlock and Zajac 3, Aungier p. 406, l. 25) for 'altar cloth', using William's sign for cloth, and adding a sign for altar or blessing. Evidently this 'cloth' sign, which in the Cluny list is used only for a type of bed-covering (no. 47), and may stand specifically for linen, was transmitted to England independently of the *Indicia*.

20. William of Hirsau's sign for 'chalice' (no. 156), adds the sign of the cross to the sign for a cup, and this is found in one of the Bury lists (Sherlock and Zajac 11); Syon uses a sign for 'cup' for 'chalice' without any augmentation (Aungier p. 406, l. 4).

---

[5] Mayo, p. 146.

William has a separate sign for 'paten' (no. 157), in which a circle is made with the thumb and fingers for its shape.

21. This sign, also found in William of Hirsau (no. 158) and the two Bury lists (Jarecki no. 3, Sherlock and Zajac 2), mimes holding the bread between finger and thumb, as the Bury description explains.

22. This differs from the signs for wine in all other lists. Cluny (no. 27) and the other continental lists have 'digitum inflecte et ita labris adiunge' (bend the finger and so put it to the lips), the sign for drinking in general, while the later English lists give a different sign again (Jarecki 6, no. 64, Sherlock and Zajac no. 13, and Aungier p. 409, 1. 31), in which the tips of thumb and forefinger are rubbed together in front of the eye.

Only in the *Indicia* and the Bury list printed by Sherlock and Zajac is wine found in the section on the church; in the continental lists and the other Bury list it is among the signs used in the refectory (the Syon list is alphabetical, so sheds no light on classification). Presumably, on the continent and later on in England, the sign was used in both places, and liturgical use was thought of as a specialized function of what was primarily a drink. The discontinuity in the nature of the sign used may also be due to the rarity of wine in English monasteries at the time of the *Indicia*. No continental sign was taken over by Anglo-Saxon monks because they had so little use for it, and their own must have fallen into disuse as well; when wine became more common in England, the memory of the earlier signs, both English and continental, had been lost.

It is interesting, too, that the English sign indicates not drinking wine, but dispensing it, as if this were the activity more familiar to English monks. However, there is considerable evidence for wine in Anglo-Saxon England, and a rather coy speech given to one of the boys in Ælfric's *Colloquy* shows that it appeared in refectories: 'non sum tam dives ut possim emere mihi vinum; et vinum non est potus puerorum sive stultorum, sed senum et sapientium' (I'm not so rich that I can buy myself wine; and wine is not a drink for boys or fools, but for the old and wise).[6] A sign for a drink based on wine does also appear in the *Indicia*'s section on food (no. 84 below).

23. A sign unique to the *Indicia*, possibly for the reasons outlined under sign 22 above. It presumably denotes the cruet, the flask in which the eucharistic wine was kept, rather than literally a horn. David Sherlock suggests that the action described is pulling the stopper from a flask.[7]

24. No sign in Cluny, but William of Hirsau has 'premisso metalli signo hoc adde, ut tribus digitis ipsum moveri paululum simules' (to the sign for metal already given, add this, that you pretend with three fingers to move it (the censer) a little - no. 162). The second half of this description corresponds roughly with the *Indicia* sign. A similar sign to William's occurs in one of the Bury lists (Sherlock and Zajac no. 18), but that in the Syon list is simpler, more like the *Indicia*'s: 'Meue thy right hande to and fro as thoughe thou shulde cense' (Aungier, p. 408, l. 39). However, the versions are not sufficiently distinct to indicate a separate transmission.

25. The holding up of the thumb indicates something large. In Cluny this is indicated with the whole hand (sign no. 86), and this appears later in England, in one of the Bury lists (Sherlock and Zajac, no. 95). William of Hirsau converts the sign for wax or candle into 'candela maior' with the instruction to squeeze the left arm with the right hand (no. 313), presumably again to indicate the size of the candle. For the basic sign for 'candle', see below, no. 27.

26. Presumably 'candelsticca' and 'candelstæf' are synonymous. Of the other lists, only Syon has a sign for candlestick, in which one fist is placed above the other (Aungier p. 406, l. 2). William of Hirsau (no. 163) and the Bury lists (no. 29 in

---

[6] Garmonsway, p. 47.

[7] Sherlock, p. 23.

Jarecki, no. 17 in Sherlock and Zajac) give signs for 'candelabrum' combining a sign for 'metal' with, in William's case, three fingers pointing downwards for its three feet, and at Bury, the sign for 'candle'.

27. Evidently a smaller candle than the taper of no. 25, but not small enough to warrant the use of the little finger. The blowing on the index finger in other lists indicates 'fire' in general; in William of Hirsau's sign for 'candle' (no. 312), it is added to the sign for 'wax' (no. 311), but this in itself mimes the making of candles. The Bury lists have the same signs for 'candle' and 'wax' (nos 25-6 in Jarecki, nos 15 and 16 in Sherlock and Zajac), but Syon has its own sign for 'candle': 'make the sign of buttur with the sign fore day' (Aungier p. 406, 1. 1).

28. The same as William of Hirsau's sign for 'lignum ad lumen tenendum compositu' (wooden object made for holding a light - no. 230), which is explained rather better: 'manum sinistram extende interiora eius sursum vertens alteramque in iunctura manus et brachii super ipsam erige, sicut vides ipsum instrumentum esse factum, et adde luminis signum' (hold out the left hand, turning its inside upwards, and raise the other on it at the joint of hand and arm, as you see this utensil is made, and add the sign of light). It may simply be a board on which a candle is stuck, perhaps in a hole or on a spike, or there may be a wooden socket sticking up to receive the candle, represented by the right hand. No other list has such a sign.

29. According to Gneuss, this is the only occurrence of this word in Old English to mean a physical book, rather than the concept of the bible. The moving of the hand indicates the turning of pages, as in the previous group of signs for books (nos 8-12), the thumb the size of what must have been by far the largest book known to the monks. The hand under the cheek means 'sleep', as in the sign for 'dormitory' (no. 87 below), and indicates the books used in the night office or matins, as explicitly stated in the Cluny list (no. 68): 'Pro signo libri in

quo legendum est ad nocturnos, premisso generale signo et libri et lectionis adde, ut manum ponas ad maxillam' (For the sign of a book which is to be read from at the night office, to the sign already given for both book and reading, add, that you put your hand to your cheek). The sign is transferred from sleep, to night, to the office, rather than meaning that the monks slept through it.[8]

Cluny has no sign for 'bible', but William of Hirsau (no. 215) adds to the sign for 'book': 'ut proferas omnes digitos utriusque manus' (that you stick out all the fingers of both hands). This may be a sign for 'all', meaning all the books of the bible, which were not normally combined into a single volume. These signs are not found in the later English lists.

30. Gneuss states that this is the legendary, containing whole *vitae* of martyrs and confessors, as opposed to the martyrology, which gave only brief notes (see no. 45). 'Hand' must be a mistake for 'throat', as in no. 45, and in signs for 'martyr', 'martyrology' in other lists (Cluny 76; Bury 41 in Jarecki, no. 59 in Sherlock and Zajac). William of Hirsau has a different sign for 'martyrology' (no. 227), involving adding up quickly on the fingers, perhaps for the great number of martyrs, or for the dates of their feasts.

31. Gneuss points out that 'godspelltraht' is used by Wærferth to mean Gregory the Great's Homiliary, and that 'traht' means 'homily' in Ælfric's usage. Christ also translates 'Homilien', but the cross on the front of the head stands for the Gospels themselves in sign 10. Only William of Hirsau has a sign for 'homiliary' (no. 219) which adds the sign for 'bishop', whose responsibility preaching was, to that for 'book'.

32. Presumably paying attention stands for the Psalter because it had to be learnt by heart. The Cluny sign for the Psalter (no. 72) uses the sign of a crown (see below, sign 118) to indicate King David who wrote the psalms. This is also the

---

[8] see Barley 1974 for semiotic aspects of the text.

sign found in the later English lists (Jarecki 6, no. 35, Sherlock and Zajac no. 47, Aungier p. 408, 1. 38).

33. The little finger because the hymnal was a slim volume, even the New Hymnal introduced from the continent in the tenth century having only a hundred hymns (Gneuss). The Cluny sign for the hymnal (no. 71) uses the sign for 'first', for the opening words 'Primo dierum', and the Bury lists use the same principle: 'extensa manu summitates indicis et pollicis coniunge ut circulus appareat ... propter primam litteram ympnarii, quod est O' (with the hand held out, join the tips of index finger and thumb, so that a circle appears ... for the first letter of the hymnal, which is O. - Jarecki 6, no. 36, Sherlock and Zajac no. 49).

34. The first part of this sign means a dish or cup, as in nos 53 and 79. Of the other lists, only William of Hirsau has a sign for lantern or lamp (no. 315): 'premisso signo iusticie signum splendoris adiunge' (to the sign for cup already given, join the sign for shining). This is evidently the same sign, and presumably from Cluny, although not in the Cluny list. Although the word 'leohtfæt' (light-vessel) is ambiguous, the use of the 'blowing on the finger' sign seems to imply a candle in the *Indicia*, and this sign should therefore mean a lantern, for protecting a candle, rather than a lamp. William's headword 'laterna' can also mean both. For 'lamp' see below, sign 88.

35-6. Presumably it is the left finger that is laid over the right, to make a physical cross, as opposed to the sign of the cross as in blessing. The Cluny list has no sign for cross, but William of Hirsau (no. 154) gives 'indice super indicem posito ipsam crucem simulabis' (you shall imitate the cross itself with index finger placed over index finger). The same sign is found in the two Bury lists (no. 27 in Jarecki, no. 19 in Sherlock and Zajac).

37. See no. 27 above for signs for 'candle' and 'candlestick'.

38. 'þu' in the first part of the sentence, and 'he' in the second, refer to the same person, the one who wants to sit down. The

sign for sitting is more or less the same as no. 40. These signs seem to be unique to the *Indicia*, although the attitude of seeking permission must have been common, even where not explicitly prescribed in a sign-list. The later English lists, however, have a different sign for 'licence', in which the hand is raised in front of the face, with the fingers pointing upwards (no. 96 in Jarecki, 6, Sherlock and Zajac no. 137, and Aungier p. 408, l. 5). The gesture for sitting is also so basic that it may well have been in use, although unrecorded.

39. The only other list with a sign for standing up is Syon: 'Meve thy hand esely vpwarde' (Aungier p. 409, l. 15). However, this is another sign that could have been in widespread use, even where there was no formal sign-language.

40. See above, no. 38, for discussion.

41. The second and third person pronouns again refer to the same individual. A sign for 'enough' is found only in the English lists, but in the later ones it is a different sign: 'clauso pugno pollicem extende' (with closed fist, stick out the thumb - no. 42 in Jarecki, no. 147 in Sherlock and Zajac, and Aungier p. 147, l. 33). This is the *Indicia* sign for 'large', which is not found with this meaning in the later lists.

42. No other list has this sign exactly, but there is a Cluny sign (no. 115) for assent, 'annuicio', in which the hand is turned palm upwards. The two Bury lists have a different sign again for 'affirmacio' (no. 49 in Jarecki, no. 143 in Sherlock and Zajac).

43. This differs from the Cluny sign (no. 116) for 'negacio', in which the middle finger is flicked away from the thumb, and which appears in all the other lists, except for Syon, which has 'Meue esely thy fyngers of thy right hande, flatlynges, and fro the, and it serueth for Nay' (Aungier p. 407, l. 28), probably the same sign as in the *Indicia*.

44. This appears to be simply a gesture of asking forgiveness, since the chapter was where one confessed ones faults to the

community, and received penance or punishment. This is made explicit by the Bury sign (no. 46) 'pro capitulo correctionis', although the sign itself is different. William of Hirsau has a sign for 'chapter-house', combining sign for 'building' and 'sin' (no. 297), which is also found in Syon (Aungier p. 406, l. 6). All three use the same idea, but the signs themselves must be of independent origin. The chapter itself was obviously not silent, but signs were presumably useful while others were speaking.

45. This is, according to Gneuss, the book now known as a martyrology, providing only brief notes on the lives and deaths of martyrs and confessors, as opposed to the larger legendary indicated by sign 30 above. The martyrology was used in the chapter office.

46. A chapter from the Rule was read at chapter (hence the name). Only the *Indicia* has this pun on the other meaning of 'regula'; Cluny has a sign (no. 70) referring to St Benedict, while the later English lists managed without one.

47-8. These two signs are unique to the *Indicia*, although it seems unlikely that corporal punishment was a special feature of Anglo-Saxon, as opposed to continental or later English, monasticism. Chapter 2 of the Rule of St Benedict advises: 'improbos autem et duros ac superbos uel inobedientes uerberum uel corporis castigatione in ipso initio peccati coerceat' (and let him (the abbot) restrain the badly behaved, and the inflexible and proud, or the disobedient, with blows or chastisement of the body, at the very beginning of their wrong-doing).

49. This sign for eating occurs with minor variations in William of Hirsau (no. 39), Syon (Aungier p. 406, l. 37) and the Bury list printed by Jarecki (no. 130).

50-1. These signs are also found only in the *Indicia*. In later monasteries the reader was provided with a pulpit.

52. Also unique to the *Indicia*.

53. This is the original Cluny sign (no. 32) 'manum latius extende'

(spread the hand out wider), which occurs in some form in all the other lists, except Syon, which has its own sign (Aungier p. 406, l. 32) showing the circular shape.

54. This is no. 1 in the Cluny list, and occurs in all the others. The continental lists also have signs for several special kinds of bread, but these are not found in the English lists, except that from Ely, following its Parisian exemplar.

55. In Cluny (no. 53) one cuts with the whole hand, and this is reflected in the later English lists (Jarecki nos 60 and 71, Sherlock and Zajac no. 67, Aungier p. 405, l. 24).

56. Literally a stick, and apparently used more like a fork, which are not thought to have been in general use until much later in the Middle Ages. None of the other lists have this sign. Skewers are seen in use in the Bayeux Tapestry, although not for eating with.[9] Martin Carver has argued that an illustration in the Harley Psalter, showing a king and queen eating, represents a single-pronged fork in the queen's hand, while the king has a knife, but it is not absolutely clear that these are two different implements.[10] The Bayeux tapestry also shows a table set for a feast (for which the food is being cooked on the skewers), where two implements are lying on the cloth. One is certainly a knife with a curved blade, but the other, which is straight, could conceivably represent a 'stycca'.[11]

57. Presumably equivalent to the Cluny sign (no. 7) 'pulmenti oleribus confecti' (a cooked dish made of vegetables), in which cutting is imitated with the fingers, as in the *Indicia* sign for 'knife'. This version is preserved in the two Bury lists (no. 100 in Jarecki, no. 76 in Sherlock and Zajac).

58. This sign seems to occur only in the *Indicia*, although Cluny has a sign (no. 24) for raw leeks, where the thumb and forefinger are joined, perhaps in imitation of picking leeks out

---

[9] see Wilson, plates 46-7.

[10] see Carver, p. 129.

[11] Wilson, plate 48.

of the ground. Leeks were by far the most common vegetable in early medieval England, so it may be that 'vegetables' effectively meant 'leeks'. However, the next sign shows that they did need to be specified sometimes. This sign, whose performance is clarified by the next one, may signify sharpness, for it is also used to indicate the thorns of sloes (sign 77). It may also be related to the Bury sign for spices, in which the palm is tapped (Jarecki no. 91, Sherlock and Zajac no. 135), which may in turn be connected with the *Indicia* signs for flavoured drinks (nos 85 and 86 below).

59. See the previous entry for the Cluny sign for leeks, and for their popularity. 'Læc' could, however, include onions and garlic. There is a sign in Cluny for 'garlic or radish' (no. 25) in which one mimes smelling, although not by the same gesture as here. The later English lists do not have this sign.

60. Pottage is made by boiling cereals, and may be flavoured with herbs and vegetables. The equivalent sign in Cluny (no. 15) is for 'milium', a kind of millet, which was probably not available in England, although the Bury lists have the sign (no. 106 in Jarecki, no. 85 in Sherlock and Zajac). In all these, stirring is mimed with the forefinger, rather than the fist as in the *Indicia*.

61. Presumably to simulate grinding, although by what means is not clear. William of Hirsau's is the only other list with a sign for pepper (no. 84): 'simula circumducentem molam' (imitate turning the mill). However, the Bury lists have a sign for flavourings in general which is evidently related: 'pugnum super pugnum quasi aliquid terendo gira addendo signum specierum quod ita fit: clauso pugno percute bis vel ter sinistram palmam interius cum extremitate dextri indicis' (turn fist over fist as if grinding something, adding the sign for spices, which is made like this: with the fist closed, hit the inside of the left palm two or three times with the tip of the right forefinger - no. 72 in Jarecki, no. 97 in Sherlock and Zajac). The *Indicia* sign could conceivably be related to this last if a word meaning 'hand' or 'palm' had been omitted.

62. This is the Cluny sign for beans (no. 5), found in all other lists except Syon, where a more refined diet may have been followed. At Cluny, and very likely elsewhere, beans were eaten every day.[12]

63. William of Hirsau's is the only other list with a sign for peas (no. 9), where the thumb is placed on the first joint not of the little finger, but the index. It is in his sign for lentils (no. 10) that the little finger is used. Presumably the choice of finger indicated the descending order of size, bean, pea, lentil. It is unlikely that lentils were known in Anglo-Saxon England, so the usual finger for smallness could be transferred to peas. These signs must go back to Cluny, even though they are not found in the list written there.

64. Another basic Cluny sign (no. 17) that is found in all the other lists. Very small cheeses must have been made, by modern standards, if they could be pressed between the hands.

65. This sign is not in the Cluny list, but appears in William of Hirsau's (no. 41), and in more or less the same form in the Syon list (Aungier p. 405, 1. 30). The two Bury lists have a different sign for 'fat', which basically refers to the human body (Jarecki no. 89, Sherlock and Zajac no. 94).

66. The Cluny sign for milk (no. 20) imitates an infant suckling, rather than milking a cow. The Bury lists do not mention milk, but Syon has 'Draw thy left litle fynger in maner of mylkyng' (Aungier p. 408, 1. 12), presumably derived from the *Indicia*. This is also the sign given by William of Hirsau (no. 31), so Cluny usage may have changed.

67. This sign is explained by its Cluny original (no. 6): 'cum digito in altero digito simula testam ovi vellicantem' (with the finger imitate picking off an egg shell on the other finger). The same sign is found in all the lists except those derived from St Victor.

68. The continental lists do not have a sign for salt. It does occur,

---

[12] Evans, p. 89.

however, in one of the Bury lists and in Syon (Sherlock and Zajac no. 102, Aungier p. 408, 1. 34). The sign is different but also mimes salting the food.

69. This is the only food signalled by reference to taste. It is a Cluny sign (no. 21), but does not appear in the later English lists.

70. Another Cluny sign (no. 8), found in all the lists. Apart from Syon, the others have a fairly long list of different fishes, which perhaps were not differentiated by the Anglo-Saxons.

71. A sign for eels appears in all lists except Syon, but the others use some form of the Cluny sign (no. 10): 'cumclude utramque manum, quasi qui ita tenet et premit anguillam' (close both hands together, like someone who holds and squeezes an eel like that). The placing of the right hand on the arm here stands for length, as in no. 12. Large numbers of eels were consumed in early medieval England: many Domesday mills, fisheries and marshes paid their rent in eels, and this is not likely to have been a Norman innovation.[13]

72. No other list has a sign for 'oyster'. This may indicate a difference in eating habits; there is ample evidence that oysters played an important part in Anglo-Saxon diet.[14]

73. This is the Cluny sign 'pomorum, maxime piri vel mali' (fruit, especially pears or apples - no. 22). William of Hirsau (no. 45) excludes pears from this classification (see next sign), and in the English lists it appears to mean apples specifically. In the two Bury lists this is uncertain, since they use the word 'pomum' (no. 111 in Jarecki, no. 90 in Sherlock and Zajac), which can also mean fruit in general, as in the Cluny list, but the Syon sign specifies 'Appull' (Aungier p. 405, 1. 9). The sign is the same throughout.

74. William of Hirsau's sign for pears (no. 46) uses only the index finger, but the later English lists use all the fingers, following

---

[13] Darby, p. 279.

[14] Ann Hagen, personal communication.

the *Indicia* (no. 76 in Jarecki, no. 91 in Sherlock and Zajac, and Aungier p. 408, l. 15).

75. The stroking along the fist presumably indicates the cleft between the two halves of a plum. William of Hirsau's is the only other list with a sign for 'plum' (no. 52), and his is quite different, involving pointing at the eyes.

76. Cluny has a sign for 'cherry' (no. 23) but this simply adds pointing to the cheek, for the red colour, to the general sign for fruit. Redness is presumably also the point of the pinching in the *Indicia* sign. The other English lists ignore cherries.

77. No other list has a sign for sloes, although William of Hirsau gives one for 'little plums' (no. 52), simply combining his 'plum' and 'small' signs. This could mean sloes, or simply smaller varieties of cultivated plum.

78. Salt meat is not specified in any other list, and only William of Hirsau (no. 40) and Syon (Aungier p. 407, l. 9) mention meat at all. Their sign involves lifting the skin of the left hand with the fingers of the right. Monks were not supposed to eat meat unless they were sick,[15] or after being bled, but it might be cooked in the monastery for guests or children; the boy in Ælfric's *Colloquy* says: 'Adhuc carnibus uescor, quia puer sum sub uirga degens' (I still eat meat, because I am a child living under the rod).[16] The fact that it was salted, however, suggests that butchery was not carried out on the premises. The isolated occurrence of this sign in the *Indicia* may mean that it represents conditions unique to Anglo-Saxon monasteries, which ceased to obtain after the Conquest.

79. This is the Cluny sign (no. 33) 'cyphi qui capit cotidianam vini mensuram' (the cup that holds the daily measure of wine) as prescribed in chapter 40 of the Benedictine Rule. Jarecki has shown that, between the dates of origin of the Cluny list and William of Hirsau's, either the wine allowance had come to be

---

[15] *RSB* chapters 36 and 39.

[16] Garmonsway, p. 46.

measured in a different vessel, the *iustitia* (William no. 100), or the name of the vessel had changed.[17] The occurrence of this word in the *Indicia* supports the view that our text is intermediate in date between the two continental lists. However, it should be noted that the Old English does not mention either measuring or wine, so it cannot be stated categorically that *iustitian* was understood as a wine measure. The sign does not seem to have been transmitted to the later English lists.

80. The shape of the left hand here does not mimic precisely any of the signs for vessels (nos 53, 79, 81 or 82), but the fact that this sign follows that for 'measure', and uses one of the same words, may indicate that this was the vessel most likely to be covered. The action of putting on the lid is the same as in the Cluny sign 'fladonum' (little cheese pies - no. 18): 'de una manu omnes digitos inflecte et ita manu cava in superficiem alterius manus pone' (bend all the fingers of one hand and with the hand curved like this place it on the palm of the other hand). No other list mentions a lid for a vessel of any kind.

81. The emendation of 'Wicelre', an error caused by the scribe, probably reading 'wilcere', inserting the wrong initial, was first pointed out by Logeman, and the use of the thumb clinches the matter. This is a bigger version of the dish in sign 53, but its occurrence among the drinking vessels, and the action of putting the index finger to the lips, shows that it was used to hold drink, not solid food.

82. This is the Cluny sign for 'patere ex qua bibitur' (cup out of which one drinks - no. 34), with the addition of signs for 'drinking' and 'small'. No sign is given in the *Indicia* for an ordinary sized drinking vessel, but one could obviously be deduced. This sign did reach the Bury lists (no. 67 in Jarecki, no. 71 in Sherlock and Zajac), but Syon has its own sign, imitating holding a cup (Aungier p. 406, 1. 26).

---

[17] Jarecki, Introduction, pp. 69-70.

83. This sign explains the touching of the lips in the previous two signs. The laying of the finger along the lips is not required by Cluny (no. 27), or in the later English lists (no. 113 in Jarecki, no. 100 in Sherlock and Zajac, Aungier p. 406, l. 35), and may perhaps be a mistake in the *Indicia*.

84. It is not at all clear what 'dripped' wine might be. The sign simply combines 'wine' with 'drip'. It would be tempting to propose 'distilled', since the spirit appears in drops from the alembic, but there is no evidence that this practice reached England before Latin translations of Arabic medical works became available, probably in the twelfth century.[18] Several words for wine reduced by evaporation were taken over from Latin into Old English, but there is no real evidence that such products were drunk in Anglo-Saxon England, and 'dripped' does not describe the process of boiling down very well.[19]

85. This appears to be similar, if not identical, to the Cluny sign 'potionis pigmentate' (for flavoured drink - no. 28): 'conclude manum et ita simula molentem' (close the hand and so mime grinding). William of Hirsau's version (no. 91) is more like the *Indicia*'s: 'conclude utramque manum et circumducentem molam simula' (close both hands and mime turning the mill). He calls the drink 'claratum'.

William's sign for 'beer' (no. 88, not in Cluny) involves blowing on the right hand, while the signs in the later English lists appear to be derived from this (no. 61 in Jarecki, nos 68-9 in Sherlock and Zajac, Aungier p. 405, l. 6). This situation seems to support, although far from conclusively, the contention that Old English 'beor' did not mean 'beer' at all, but some kind of fruit-flavoured drink.[20] However, there is evidence that beer was consumed in Anglo-Saxon monasteries: the boy in Ælfric's *Colloquy*, who didn't consider himself old

---

[18] see Talbot for the development of medieval English medical knowledge.

[19] see Fell 1981 for a discussion of these loan-words.

[20] see Fell 1975 for an examination of the evidence on this point.

or wise enough to drink wine, drank water or beer instead: 'Ceruisam, si habeo, uel aquam si non habeo ceruisam' (Beer, if I have any, or water if I haven't any beer).[21]

86. Whatever the original head-word for this sign was, the scribe interpreted it as something to do with the dormitory. 'Burhreste' should mean 'rest in a private bedroom'. However, the sign itself, combining elements meaning 'vegetable/herb/spice' and 'drink', clearly belongs in the section on the refectory.[22] Barley suggests that the head-word should read 'beordræst' (dregs of 'beor', for which see the previous sign), but it seems to me unlikely that such a commodity would be consumed in the refectory, or that such a concept would be represented by this combination of signs. The two elements of the sign in Old English are 'wyrt' and 'drenc', forming a compound 'wyrtdrenc' that is common in the Old English medical texts, where numerous recipes for such preparations are found.[23]

Even if spelt 'wurt-', this word shares few letters with 'burhreste', so we must assume that the exemplar was extremely illegible at this point, and that the scribe, before reading the description of the sign, was misled by the contents of the following entries. The word 'fyst' in this entry is written over an erasure, suggesting that the scribe was expecting to describe a different action, but all attempts to discover what lies underneath have failed. It is unlikely that two signs, one for 'wyrtdrenc' and one for 'burhreste', have been conflated, since the next sign, for 'dormitory' is the logical first entry of a section covering sleeping and clothing.

'Wyrtdrenc' would appear to be equivalent to 'potio pigmentata' (see previous entry), and although the *Indicia* sign does not seem to correspond well with that sign in the Cluny list, it is more like William of Hirsau's version (no. 91), in

---

[21] Garmonsway, p. 47.

[22] as pointed out in print by Barley, 1977.

[23] e.g. Cockayne, vol. 2, p. 94 (Bald's Leechbook, Book 2, chapter 16).

which he adds the sign for wine or drinking. Although the wording is quite different, it may be that *Indicia* signs 85-6 in fact describe the same action. If so, the addition to no. 86 of the sign for drinking does not seem a very good way of distinguishing two entities which, whatever else they are, are both drinks.

87. This is the Cluny sign for sleep, used to indicate the books used in the night office (no. 68). No sign for the building itself is given in Cluny, but William of Hirsau has one combining signs for building and sleep (no. 299). The same sign is found in the later English lists (no. 53 in Jarecki, no. 177 in Sherlock and Zajac, Aungier p. 406, l. 34)

88. The circle is to be drawn on the ground if nothing else is available. The wet finger is presumably to avoid burning when setting the wick of a real lamp. This sign clearly refers to a lamp, in which a wick floats in oil or grease, rather than a lantern, as in sign 34. Presumably lamps were used in the dormitory, lanterns for lighting one's way to church for the night office. This sign is not found in any other list.

89. 'Reaf' means literally 'garment', but the context, and the fact that night-clothes were unknown in the Middle Ages, show that this sign means 'bedcover'. It is not, however, the same as any of Cluny's three signs for different bed-coverings (nos 45-7), all formed on a general sign miming pulling the cover up over one's shoulder. In the two Bury lists there is still only one sign for a bedcover (no. 118 in Jarecki, no. 190 in Sherlock and Zajac), but it is the general sign from Cluny, not the *Indicia*'s.

90. Cluny has a different sign for pillow (no. 48), combining a sign for flying with that for sleep, which is reproduced in the two Bury lists (Jarecki no. 118, Sherlock and Zajac no. 192). For a feather used as a pen, see below, no. 117.

91-3. The distinctions between these three types of foot covering are not clear. 'Swyftlere', from Latin 'subtalaris', means 'sandal' or 'slipper', 'socca', according to its sign, should be a bigger version of this, and 'sceo' is Modern English 'shoe', presumably the monks' day-shoes. Cluny also has three signs for footwear (nos 42-3), 'calcei' (shoes), 'calcei nocturnales' and 'pedulia', which are marked by touching the sleeve of the frock to show they are made of wool. The signs are quite different to those in the *Indicia*, but they may indicate the same three categories: 'sceo' = 'calceus', the unmarked form, 'swyftlere' = 'calceus nocturnalis', probably light slippers, and 'socca' = 'pedule', a heavier form of the same made of wool, probably worn on winter nights. William of Hirsau's heading 'Pro signo pedulium, id est soccorum' (no. 121) confirms this last identification. Footwear is conspicuous by its absence from later English sign language, only one of the Bury lists having a sign for shoes (Sherlock and Zajac no. 185), different from those in both Cluny and the *Indicia*.

94. It is quite clear what this sign stands for, but not what its headword should be. Obviously the scribe who should have inserted the initial had no idea. Logeman proposes an 'R', giving 'rynatun', where the first element would be cognate with Old English 'run' and indicate secrecy, hence my translation 'privy'. However, there is also an Old English 'ryne', meaning a course, including a water-course. There is no firm evidence for running water in Anglo-Saxon monasteries, but the famous plan in the Eadwine Psalter of the water supply and drains at Christ Church is only about a century later than the *Indicia*.[24] There, at least, some of the elaborate system shown could already have been in existence before the Conquest.

Cluny does not have a sign for 'necessarium', and in William of Hirsau's (no. 300), the forefinger is moved downwards over the belly, rather than the whole hand. In the later lists (Sherlock and Zajac no. 198, Aungier p. 408, l. 24) this has become a sign for (male) urination, in which one shakes the clothing at the groin.

---

[24] Trinity College, Cambridge, ms. R. 17. 1. A reproduction may conveniently be found in Kauffmann, plate 181.

95. No other list has a sign for bath-house. The continental lists only have a sign for washing feet, the quintessential act of charity (Cluny no. 111), and, of the other English lists, only Syon has one for washing (Aungier p. 409, l. 26), which mimes washing the hands, like the next sign but one in the *Indicia*. One of the Bury lists includes washing with its sign for water (see no. 97 below).
96. The sign for washing the head is also unique to the *Indicia*.
97. Cluny has a different sign for water: 'omnes digitos coniuge et per obliqum move' (join all the fingers together and move them on the slant - no. 26). This reappears in one Bury list (Sherlock and Zajac no. 12), and, in modified form, Syon 'Joyne thy fyngers of thy right hande, and meve them dounward droppyngly' (Aungier p. 409, l. 24). The *Indicia* sign is more like the Syon sign for washing (see no. 95 above).
98. No other list has a sign for 'soap'.
99. Although it is called, literally, a nail-knife, this is clearly in fact a razor. Whether the same instrument was used for both cutting the nails and shaving, or whether it had changed its function without changing its name, is not apparent. Cluny has no sign for razor, but William of Hirsau gives one very like the *Indicia*'s, combining the usual sign for knife with miming shaving with a bent finger (no. 325). The shaving part of this is found in one of the Bury lists (no. 149 in Sherlock and Zajac), but none of the other English lists give a sign for 'razor'.
100. The Cluny original specifies that three fingers are to be used in this sign (no. 55), and the Bury lists use four (no. 65 in Jarecki, no. 198 in Sherlock and Zajac).
101. The Cluny sign for 'staminia' (woollen shirt - no. 36), which survives in more or less the same form in the Bury lists (no. 114 in Jarecki, no. 180 in Sherlock and Zajac).
102. Another standard sign, in Cluny (no. 37) and the Bury lists (Jarecki no. 115, Sherlock and Zajac no. 179), executed apparently with only one hand. Presumably absent from the

Syon list because nuns wore some other form of underwear.

103. Equivalent to William of Hirsau's sign (no. 124) for 'fasciolae' (leg bands): 'item digito digitum ac deinde utrumque indicem tibie circumferas' (put the finger round the finger again, and then both forefingers round the shin).

104. Evidently a covering for the lower leg, as opposed to the 'brecan' which covered the thighs. Not found in other lists.

105. This emendation was proposed by Swaen, supported by references from Ducange, without recourse to the other sign lists. The pelisse was a garment made of sheepskin or lined with fur.[25] This sign is apparently a combination of the Cluny signs for 'pellicium' (no. 41) and for 'froccus' (frock or tunic - no. 38). The first reads 'de una manu omnes digitos expande et ita in pectore positos contrahe, quasi qui lanam constringit' (spread out all the fingers on one hand and so, with them placed on the chest, bring them together, like someone squeezing wool) and the second 'manicam eius tene eodem modo, quo manica staminee est tenenda' (take hold of its sleeve in the same way that the sleeve of the shirt is to be taken hold of) (see no. 101 above). The *Indicia* has no sign for tunic, so presumably the pelisse was worn straight over the shirt by Anglo-Saxon monks.

106. Equivalent to the Cluny sign (no. 39) for 'cuculla': 'hoc adde, ut cum duobus digitis retro tangas capellam' (add this (to touching the sleeve), that you touch the hood at the back with two fingers). In the Bury lists, the same sign is found (Jarecki no. 117, Sherlock and Zajac no. 187). The cowl did not consist just of the hood, however, but also of the cape to which it was attached.[26] The use of this sign to denote a monk (no. 121) shows that it was a distinctively monastic garment. As with the liturgical vestments, the signs for the habit seem to be listed in the order in which they would be put on.

---

[25] Mayo, p. 140, under 'cassock'.

[26] Mayo, p. 147.

107. The scapular was an outer garment worn when engaged in manual labour.[27] It is generally considered to be sleeveless, but the description of this sign shows that it had sleeves of some sort at the time of the *Indicia*. There is no sign for it in the continental lists, no doubt because, as Mayo states, it was not adopted by the Cluniacs, nor does it appear in later English sign language.

108. No other list has a sign for gloves.

109. Other lists do not have signs for 'scissors', but the two Bury lists have one for 'abscissio capillorum' (cutting of hair) which corresponds to the second possibility here (no. 43 in Jarecki, no. 147 in Sherlock and Zajac).

110. The Cluny sign (no. 51) for needle is not identical, but likewise mimes sewing. It reappears in the two Bury lists (Jarecki no. 90, Sherlock and Zajac no. 196).

111. No other list has a sign for the bakehouse. The missing verb may well be something more specific than 'make', such as 'push' or 'pull'; in any case, the intention is clearly to mime kneading. It is not clear why this sign appears in the middle of hand-tools of various kinds.

112. The Cluny sign for 'stylus' (no. 57) combines the sign for metal with miming writing; it is found again in the two Bury lists (Jarecki no. 124, Sherlock and Zajac no. 133). The pointing in the *Indicia* sign, which is not found elsewhere, presumably indicates the shape of the instrument.

113. The same as the Cluny sign (no. 56) for 'tabulae', which reappears in the two Bury lists, with optional additions meaning 'wood' or 'wax' (no. 123 in Jarecki, no. 131 in Sherlock and Zajac). The tablets were made in hinged pairs, hence the sign. Stylus and tablets were used for all everyday writing; ink and parchment were reserved for important documents that were to be kept for posterity.

---

[27] Mayo, p. 33.

114. This sign is not in the other lists. It appears to indicate a tablet too large to be attached to another one. The placing of the right hand on the left arm may indicate the length of the tablet, as in sign 12, for a rectangular book.

115. No other list has this sign; their signs for 'regula' indicate that of St Benedict (see no. 46 above).

116. This sign is unique to the *Indicia*, although William of Hirsau has one for 'ink', combining those for 'water' and 'writing' (no. 318).

117. This sign does not appear in any other list. It is not clear whether it applies only to pens made from feathers, or whether the same sign could include those made from reeds.

118. Other lists do not have this sign explicitly, but it is implied in the Cluny sign for 'Psalter' (no. 72), in which the same action signifies King David (see no. 32 above).

119. A combination of the previous sign and that for 'woman' (no. 127 below).

120. Not found in the other lists. Syon has a different sign: 'Holde vp thy right haund streght ouere thy frount and hede' (Aungier p. 405, l. 32), while William of Hirsau's sign for the altar of a bishop combines signs for altar, pallium and crozier, all themselves compound signs (no. 149).

121. This is the Cluny sign (no. 80): 'cum manu tene capellum cuculle' (take hold of the hood of the cowl with the hand). It is found in the two Bury lists (Jarecki no. 126, Sherlock and Zajac no. 119).

122. This sign is unique to the *Indicia*, although made on analogy with the other Cluny signs for persons. Cluny uses the sign for woman for 'sacra virgo' (no. 78), and variations on this are used by Syon and one of the Bury lists (Aungier p. 409, l. 18 and Jarecki no. 125) to make the distinction from a laywoman.

123. A subdivision of the Cluny sign for 'clericus' (no. 81), which would include those in minor orders (see next sign), and reads: 'digitum auri circumfer quasi girando propter similitudinem corone, quam in capite clericus habet' (move the finger round

the ear as if making a circle for a likeness of the crown that the cleric has on his head). Drawing a circle round the ear does not seem a very clear way of indicating the tonsure. In the Bury lists, the circle has migrated to the cheek (Jarecki no. 48, Sherlock and Zajac no. 152), and it is clear from sign 125 below that this was where it was made in the *Indicia* too. Syon has a sign for a priest, which, since it starts with the sign for 'brother', presumably means a priest who is a monk (Aungier p. 408, l. 21): 'Make the signe of a broder, and put thy fore fynger on thyne ere and breste, or els make a cercle therwith upone thyn hede'. The circle has now reached its logical position. It is not clear why this sign uses a blessing to distinguish a priest who is not a monk from one who is, nor whether a situation is envisaged where one might specifically wish for a secular priest, or 'Gyf þu ... habban wille' is merely elegant variation.

124. This sign, evidently another subset of the Cluny 'clericus' (see previous sign), and listed between the two signs for priest, must mean not 'dean', as in sign 2 above, but 'deacon', the order next below that of priest, who assisted at the mass. He read the Gospel, hence the use of the cross on the forehead (see no. 10 above). 'eal gelice' presumably means in the form of a circle, as in the previous sign. The later English lists also denote the deacon by the cross on the forehead (Jarecki no. 14, Sherlock and Zajac no. 111, Aungier p. 406, l. 30).

125. The designation of this sign must mean that a priest who was not a monk (sign 123 above) was not necessarily celibate at this date, despite all the exhortations of the ecclesiastical hierarchy. The sign in Syon (Aungier p. 408, l. 21, see no. 123) presumably indicates a celibate priest, as here.

126. This is the Cluny sign (no. 82), explained 'quam antiquitus non raserunt id genus hominum' (because in antiquity this kind of man did not shave). It is also found in the Bury list edited by Sherlock and Zajac (no. 153).

127. The Cluny sign for 'woman' (no. 78), although there it is not confined to laywomen. It occurs in Jarecki's Bury list, again under the guise of a holy virgin (no. 125), and in Syon (Aungier p. 409, l. 34).

BIBLIOGRAPHY

Aungier, G. J.
History and Antiquities of Syon Monastery, London, 1840.

Barakat, Robert A.
The Cistercian Sign Language, Cistercian Studies Series, 11, Kalamazoo, 1975.

Barley, Nigel
'Two Anglo-Saxon Sign Systems Compared', *Semiotica,* 12 (1974), pp. 227-37.
'Two Emendations to the *Indicia Monasterialia',* *Neuphilologische Mitteilungen,* 78 (1977), pp. 326-7.

Battiscombe, C. F., ed.,
The Relics of St Cuthbert, Durham, 1956.

Brooks, Nicholas
The Early History of the Church of Canterbury, Leicester, 1984.

Carver, M. O. H.
'Contemporary Artefacts Illustrated in Late Saxon Manuscripts', *Archaeologia,* 108 (1986), pp. 117-45.

Christ, Karl
'In Caput Quadragesimae', *Zentralblatt für Bibliothekswesen,* 60 (1943), pp. 33-59.

Cockayne, T. O.
Leechdoms, Wort-cunning and Starcraft of Early England, volume 2, Rolls Series, London, 1865.

Darby, H. C.
Domesday England, Cambridge, 1977.

Dodwell, C. R.
The Canterbury School, Cambridge, 1954.

Evans, Joan
Monastic Life at Cluny 910-1157, Oxford, 1931.

Fell, Christine
'Old English *beor*', *Leed Studies in English*, new series, 8 (1975),
pp.76-95.
'A note on Old English Wine Terminology: the problem of
cæren', *Nottingham Medieval Studies*, 25 (1981), pp. 1-12.

Foot, S. R. I.
Anglo-Saxon Minsters AD 597 - ca. 900 (Cambridge PhD
dissertation), 1990.

Garmonsway, G. N.
Ælfric's Colloquy, London, 1939.

Gneuss, Helmut
'Liturgical Books in Anglo-Saxon England and their Old English
Terminology', in Michael Lapidge and Helmut Gneuss, eds,
Learning and Literature in Anglo-Saxon England, Cambridge,
1985, pp. 91-141.

Gougaud, Louis
'Le langage de silencieux', *Revue Mabillon*, 19 (1929),
pp. 93-100.

Jarecki, Walter
Signa Loquendi, Saecula Spiritalia, 4, Baden-Baden, 1981.

John of Salerno
Vita Odonis, pted Migne, Patrologia Latina, 133.

Kauffmann, C. M.
Romanesque Manuscripts 1066-1190, A Survey of Manuscripts
Illuminated in the British Isles, 3, London, 1975.

Ker, N. R.
Catalogue of Manuscripts containing Anglo-Saxon, Oxford, 1957.

Kluge, F.
'Zur Geschichte der Zeichensprache. Angelsächsische Indicia
Monasterialia', *Techmers Internationale Zeitschrift für allgemeine
Sprachwissenschaft*, 2, 1885, pp. 116-40.

Logeman, Willem S.
'Zu den "Indicia Monasterialia"', *Englische Studien*, 12 (1899), pp. 305-7.

Mayo, Janet
A History of Ecclesiastical Dress, London, 1984.

Regularis Concordia, edited by Dom Thomas Symons, London, 1953.

RSB = *Benedicti Regula*, ed. Rudolph Hanslik, Corpus Scriptorum Ecclesiasticorum Latinorum, 75, Vienna, 1960.

Schlutter, Otto B.
'Weitere Beiträge zur Altenglischen Forschungen. Bemerk-ungen zum NED.', *Anglia*, 46 (1922), pp. 323-43.

Sherlock, D.
'Anglo-Saxon Monastic Sign Language at Christ Church, Canterbury', *Archaeologia Cantiana*, 107, 1989, pp.1-27.

Sherlock, D., and W. Zajac
'Monastic Sign-Language at Bury St Edmunds in the 14th Century', *Proceedings of the Suffolk Institute of Archaeology and History*, 36, 1988, pp. 251-73.

Stevenson, W. H.
Early Scholastic Colloquies, Oxford, 1929.

Swaen, A. E. H.
'Note on the Anglo-Saxon Indicia Monasterialia', *Archiv*, 140 (1920), pp. 106-7.

Talbot, C. H.
Medicine in Medieval England, London, 1967.

Temple, E.
Anglo-Saxon Manuscripts 900-1066, A Survey of Manuscripts Illuminated in the British Isles, 2, London, 1976.

van Rijnberk, Gerard
Le Langage par Signes chez les Moines, Amsterdam, 1954

Wilson, D. M., ed.,
The Bayeux Tapestry, London, 1985.

Debby Banham

Debby Banham was born in 1953 in London and educated there and at Monkton Wyld School, Dorset. After working as an agricultural labourer, antique restorer, bookseller, graphic artist, mother, playleader, poet and typist, she read Anglo-Saxon, Norse and Celtic and then Archaeology at Cambridge, where she also wrote her PhD thesis on Anglo-Saxon Food Plants. She has a grown-up son and is a freelance writer and teacher in Cambridge.

Beowulf: Text and Translation

Translated by John Porter

The verse in which the story unfolds is, by common consent, the finest
writing surviving in Old English, a text that all students of the language
and many general readers will want to tackle in the original form. To
aid understanding of the Old English, a **literal word-by-word
translation** by John Porter is printed opposite an edited text and
provides a practical key to this Anglo-Saxon masterpiece.

UK £7·95 net   ISBN 0–9516209–2–4   192pp

Monasteriales Indicia
The Anglo-Saxon Monastic Sign Language

Edited with notes and translation by
Debby Banham

The *Monasteriales Indicia* is one of very few texts which let us see
how life was really lived in monasteries in the early Middle Ages.
Written in Old English and preserved in a manuscript of the mid-
eleventh century, it consists of 127 signs used by Anglo-Saxon monks
during the times when the Benedictine Rule forbade them to speak.
These indicate the foods the monks ate, the clothes they wore, and the
books they used in church and chapter, as well as the tools they used in
their daily life, and persons they might meet both in the monastery and
outside. The text is printed here with a parallel translation. The
introduction gives a summary of the background, both historical and
textual, as well as a brief look at the later evidence for monastic sign
language in England. Extensive notes provide the reader with details of
textual relationships, explore problems of interpretation, and set out the
historical implications of the text.

UK £6·95 net   ISBN 0–9516209–4–0   96pp

The Battle of Maldon:
Text and Translation

Translated and edited by Bill Griffiths

The Battle of Maldon was fought between the men of Essex and the Vikings in AD 991. The action was captured in an Anglo-Saxon poem whose vividness and heroic spirit has fascinated readers and scholars for generations. *The Battle of Maldon* includes the source text; edited text; parallel literal translation; verse translation; review of 86 books and articles.

UK £6·95 net   ISBN 0–9516209–0–8   96pp

Wordcraft

Concise English/Old English Dictionary and Thesaurus

Stephen Pollington

This book provides Old English equivalents to the commoner modern words in both dictionary and thesaurus formats.

UK £7·95 net   ISBN 1–898281–02–5   224pp

Alfred's Metres of Boethius

Edited by Bill Griffiths

In this new edition of the Old English *Metres of Boethius*, clarity of text, informative notes and a helpful glossary have been a priority, for this is one of the most approachable of Old English verse texts, lucid and delightful; its relative neglect by specialists will mean this text will come as a new experience to many practised students of the language; while its clear, expositional verse style makes it an ideal starting point for all amateurs of the period.

UK £12·95 net   ISBN 0–9516209–5–9   212pp

Anglo-Saxon Verse Charms, Maxims and Heroic Legends

Louis J Rodrigues

The Germanic tribes who settled in Britain during the fifth and early sixth centuries brought with them a store of heroic and folk traditions: folk-tales, legends, rune-lore, magic charms, herbal cures, and the homely wisdom of experience enshrined in maxims and gnomic verse. In the lays composed and sung by their minstrels at banquets, they recalled the glories of long-dead heroes belonging to their Continental past. They carved crude runic inscriptions on a variety of objects including memorial stones, utensils, and weapons. In rude, non-aristocratic, verse, they chanted their pagan charms to protect their fields against infertility, and their bodies against the rigours of rheumatic winters. And, in times of danger, they relied on the gnomic wisdom of their ancestors for help and guidance.

Louis Rodrigues looks at those heroic and folk traditions that were recorded in verse, and which have managed to survive the depredations of time.

UK £7·95 net   ISBN 1–898281–01–7   176pp

A Handbook of Anglo-Saxon Food: Processing and Consumption

Ann Hagen

For the first time information from various sources has been brought together in order to build up a picture of how food was grown, conserved, prepared and eaten during the period from the beginning of the 5th century to the 11th century. No specialist knowledge of the Anglo-Saxon period or language is needed, and many people will find it fascinating for the views it gives of an important aspect of Anglo-Saxon life and culture. In addition to Anglo-Saxon England the Celtic west of Britain is also covered.

UK £7·95 net   ISBN 0-9516209-8-3   192pp

Spellcraft
Old English Heroic Legends
Kathleen Herbert

The author has taken the skeletons of ancient Germanic legends about great kings, queens and heroes, and put flesh on them. Kathleen Herbert's extensive knowledge of the period is reflected in the wealth of detail she brings to these tales of adventure, passion, bloodshed and magic.

The book is in two parts. First are the stories that originate deep in the past, yet because they have not been hackneyed, they are still strange and enchanting. After that there is a selection of the source material, with information about where it can be found and some discussion about how it can be used. The purpose of the work is to bring pleasure to those studying Old English literature and, more importantly, to bring to the attention of a wider public the wealth of material that has yet to be tapped by modern writers, composers and artists.

Kathleen Herbert is the author of a trilogy, set in sixth century Britain, that includes a winner of the Georgette Heyer prize for an outstanding historical novel.

UK £6·95 net   ISBN 0–9516209–9–1   288pp

The Service of Prime
from the Old English Benedictine Office:
Text and Translation prepared by Bill Griffiths

UK £2·50 net   ISBN 0–9516209–3–2   40pp

For a full list of publications send a s.a.e. to:

Anglo-Saxon Books, 25 Malpas Drive, Pinner, Middlesex. HA5 1DQ

Tel: 081-868 1564

Available in North America from:

Paul & Company Publishers Consortium Inc.
c/o PCS Data Processing Inc., 360 West 31 St., New York, NY 1001

Þa Engliscan Gesiðas

Þa Engliscan Gesiðas (The English Companions) is a historical and cultural society exclusively devoted to Anglo-Saxon history. Its aims are to bridge the gap between scholars and non-experts, and to bring together all those with an interest in the Anglo-Saxon period, its language, culture and traditions, so as to promote a wider interest in, and knowledge of all things Anglo-Saxon. The Fellowship publishes a journal, *Wiðowinde,* which helps members to keep in touch with current thinking on topics from art and archaeology to heathenism and Early English Christianity. The Fellowship enables like-minded people to keep in contact by publicising conferences, courses and meetings that might be of interest to its members. A correspondence course in Old English is also available.

For further details write to:

Janet Goldsbrough-Jones, 38 Cranworth Road,
Worthing, West Sussex, BN11 2JF, England.

Regia Anglorum

Regia Anglorum is a society that was founded to accurately re-create the life of the British people as it was around the time of the Norman Conquest. Our work has a strong educational slant and we consider authenticity to be of prime importance. We prefer, where possible, to work from archaeological materials and are extremely cautious regarding such things as the interpretation of styles depicted in manuscripts. Approximately twenty-five per cent of our membership, of over 500 people, are archaeologists or historians.

The Society has a large working Living History Exhibit, teaching and exhibiting more than twenty crafts in an authentic environment. We own a forty foot wooden ship replica of a type that would have been a common sight in Northern European waters around the turn of the first millennium AD. Battle re-enactment is another aspect of our activities, often involving 200 or more warriors.

For further information contact:

K. J. Siddorn, 9 Durleigh Close, Headley Park,
Bristol BS13 7NQ, England.

The International Society of Anglo-Saxonists

The International Society of Anglo-Saxonists (ISAS) is an organization open to all persons interested in any aspect of the culture of Anglo-Saxon England. ISAS intends to provide scholars interested in the languages, literatures, arts, history, and material culture of *Anglo-Saxon England* with support in their research and to encourage exchanges of ideas and materials within and between disciplines. All of this is accomplished primarily through biennial meetings of the Society during which members present papers and discuss topics of mutual interest. Many of the papers appear in a revised form in *Anglo-Saxon England.*

Benefits of membership include discount subscriptions to *Anglo-Saxon England* and other publications. Only members of the Society can attend and present papers at its meetings.

To join ISAS contact:

Patrick W. Conner, ISAS, Dept. of English, 231 Stansbury Hall, West Virginia University, Morgantown, WV26506, USA.

Old English Newsletter

The *OEN* is a journal produced by, and for, scholars of Old English. It is a refereed periodical. Solicited and unsolicited manuscripts (except for independent reports and news items) are reviewed by specialists in anonymous reports. Four issues are published each (American) academic year for the Old English Division of the Modern Language Association by the Centre for Medieval and Early Renaissance Studies at the State University of New York at Binghamton.

General correspondence should be addressed to the Editor:

Paul E. Szarmach, CEMERS; SUNY-Binghamton, PO Box 6000, Binghamton, New York 13902-6000, USA.